Real World
Colouring Book
For Advanced Users & Adults

50 Images

**Created From Real Life Photos
For You To Colour As You Please.**

ISBN 978-0-359-86515-4
90000
9 780359 865154

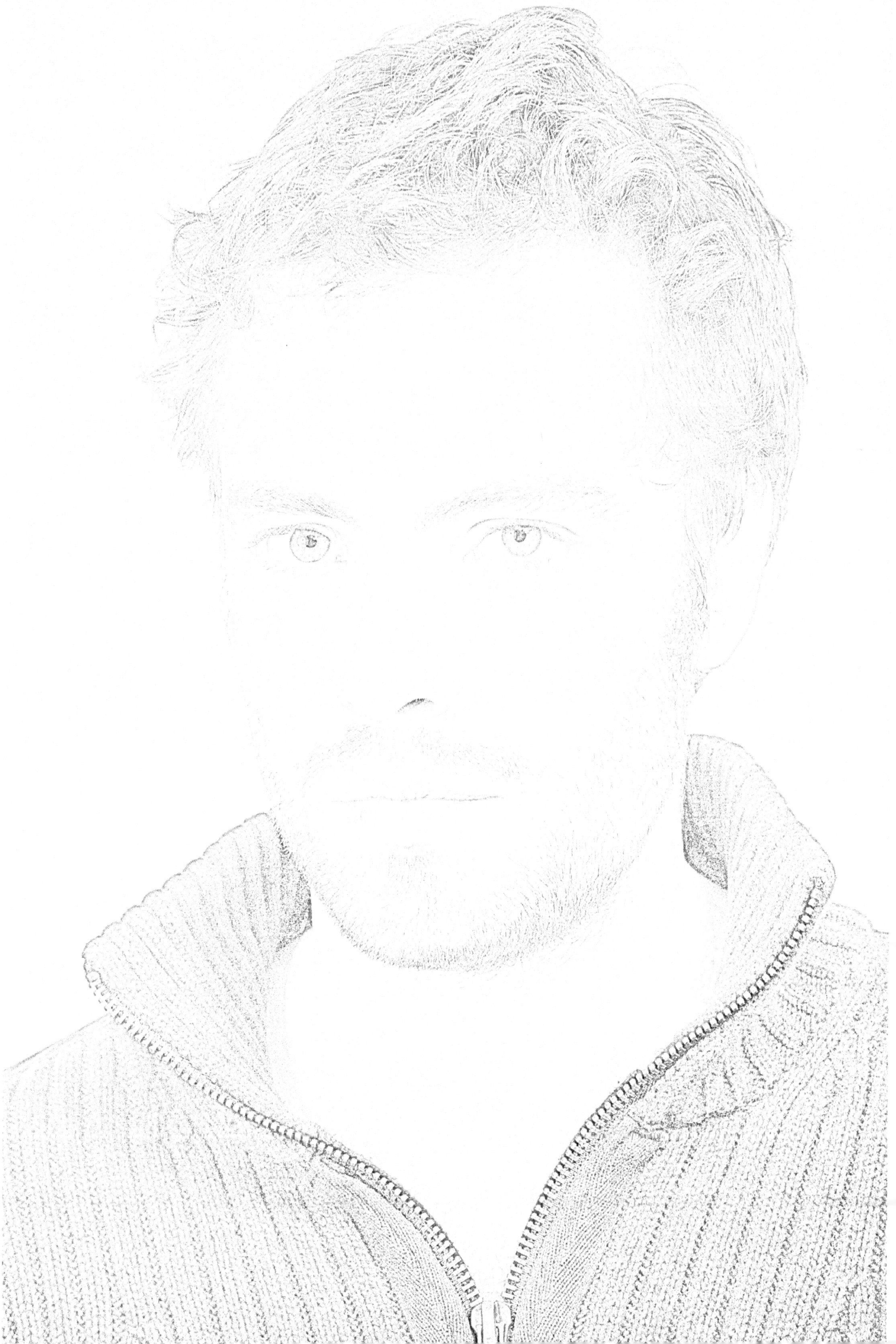

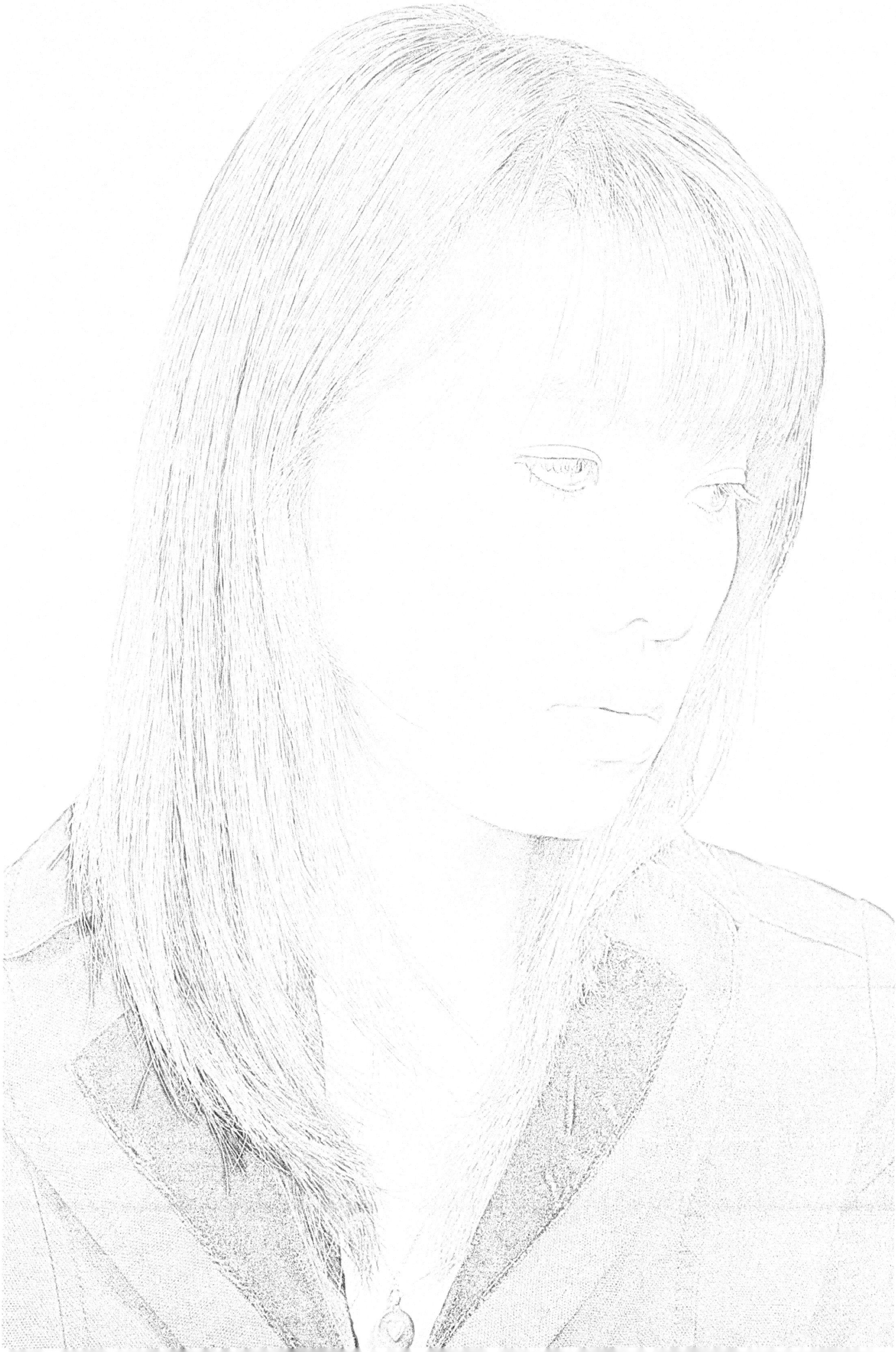

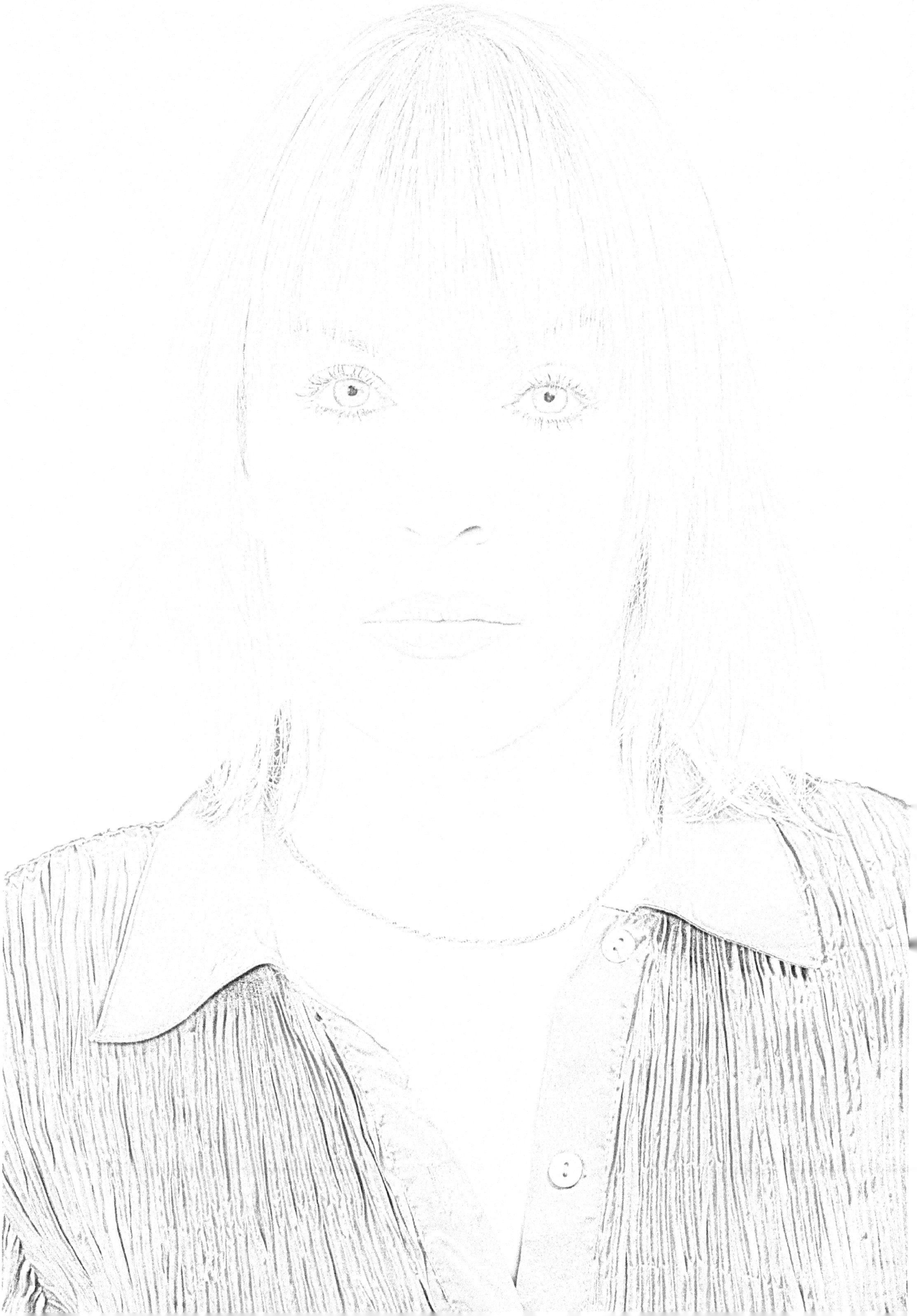

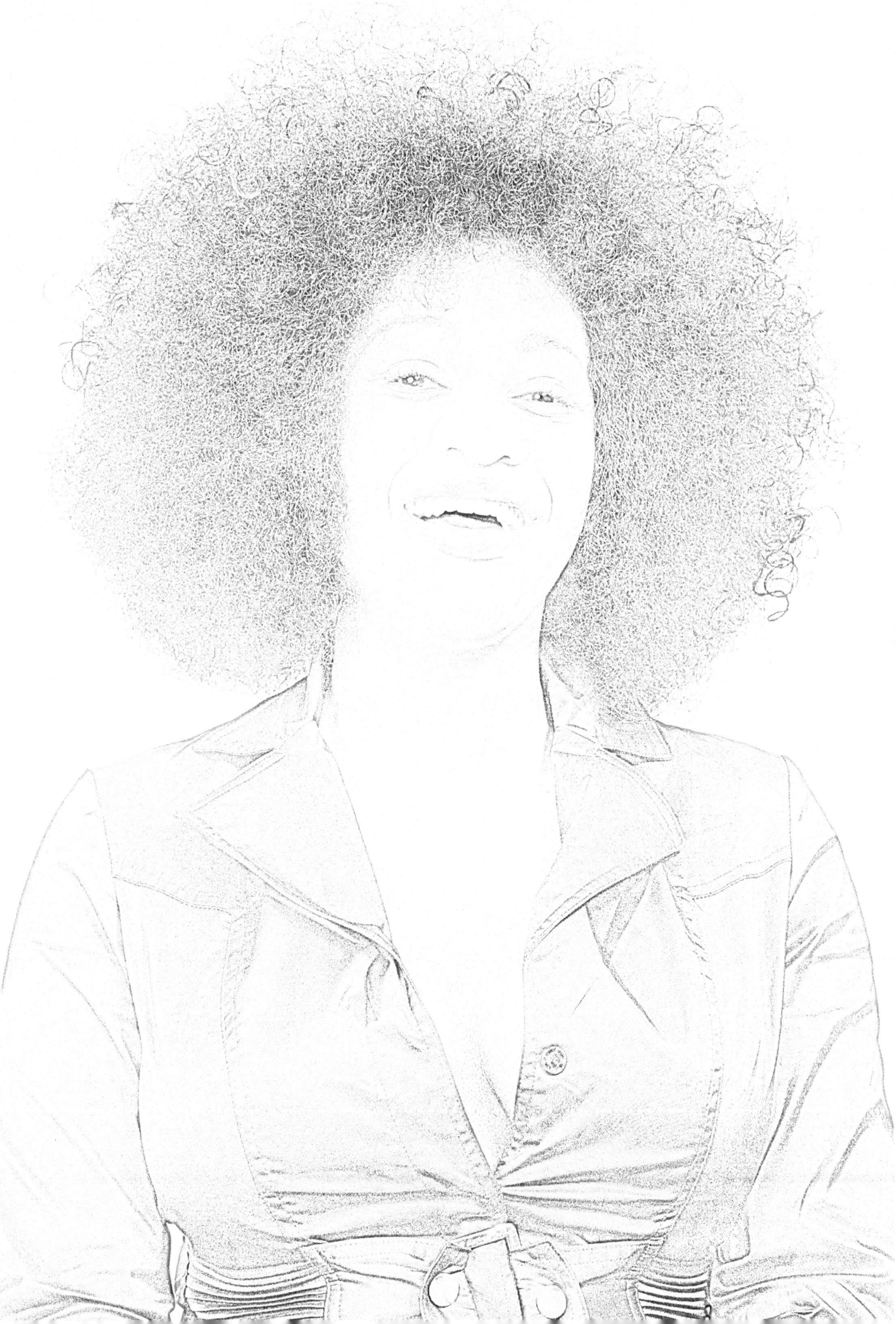

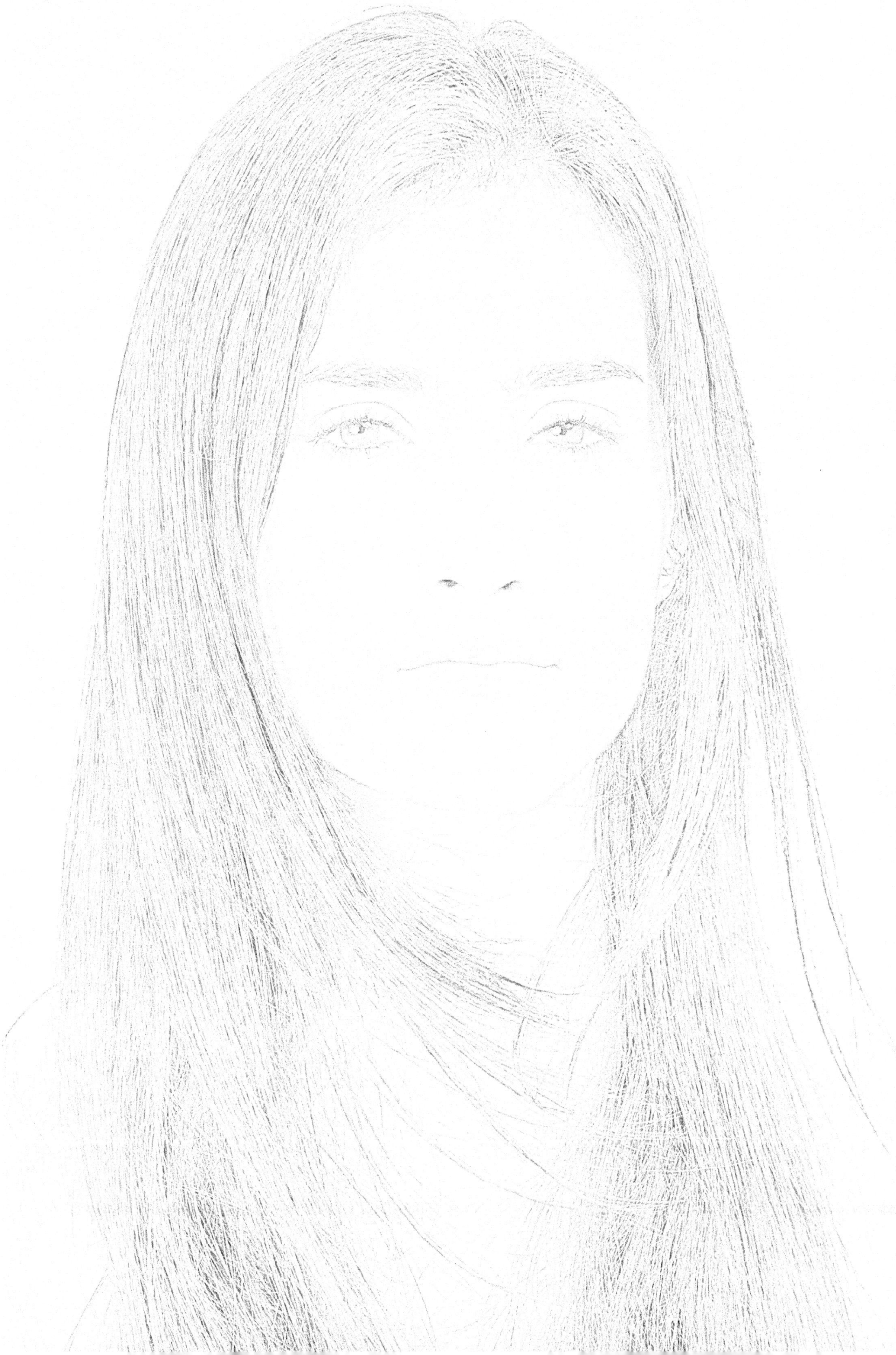

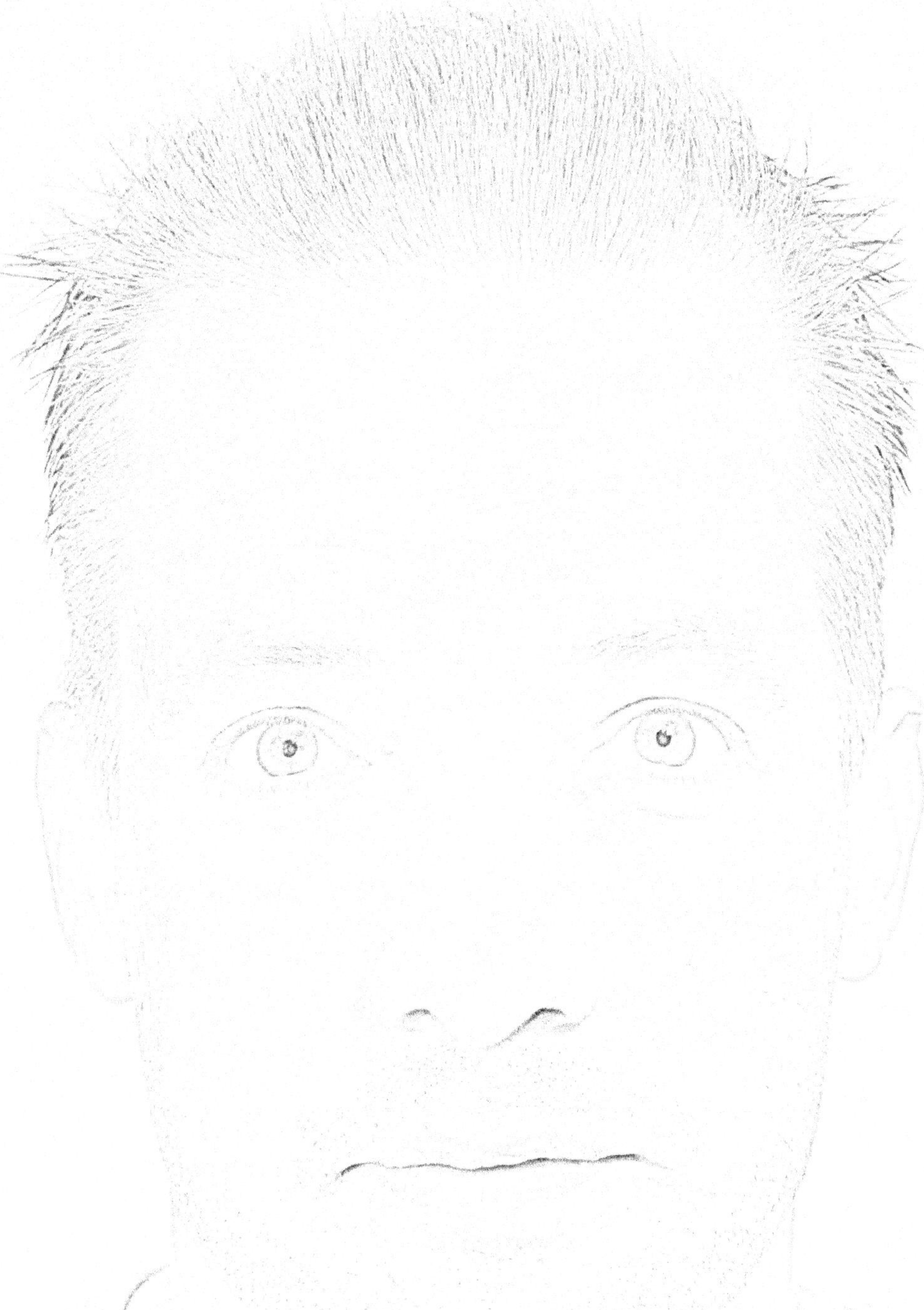

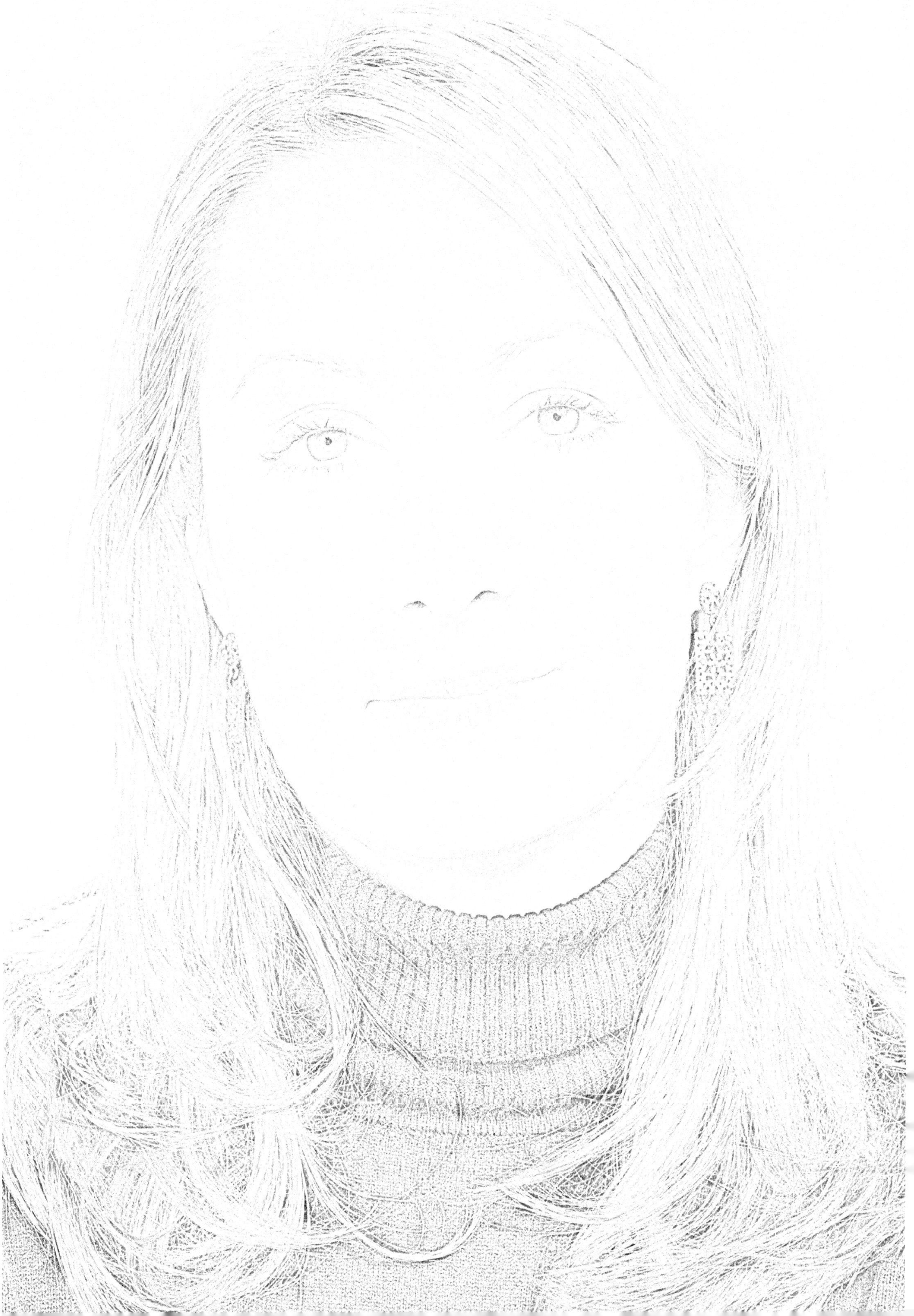

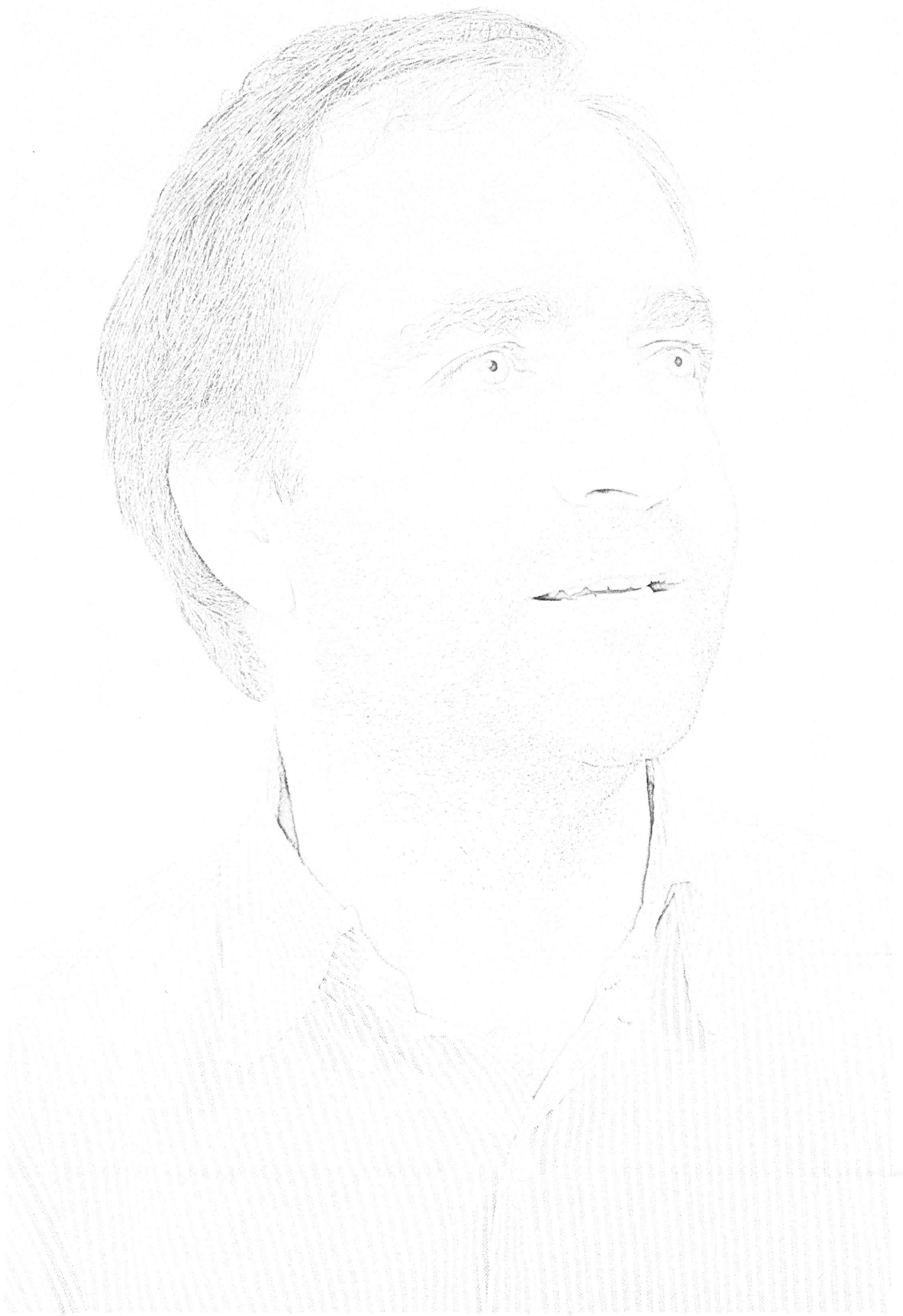

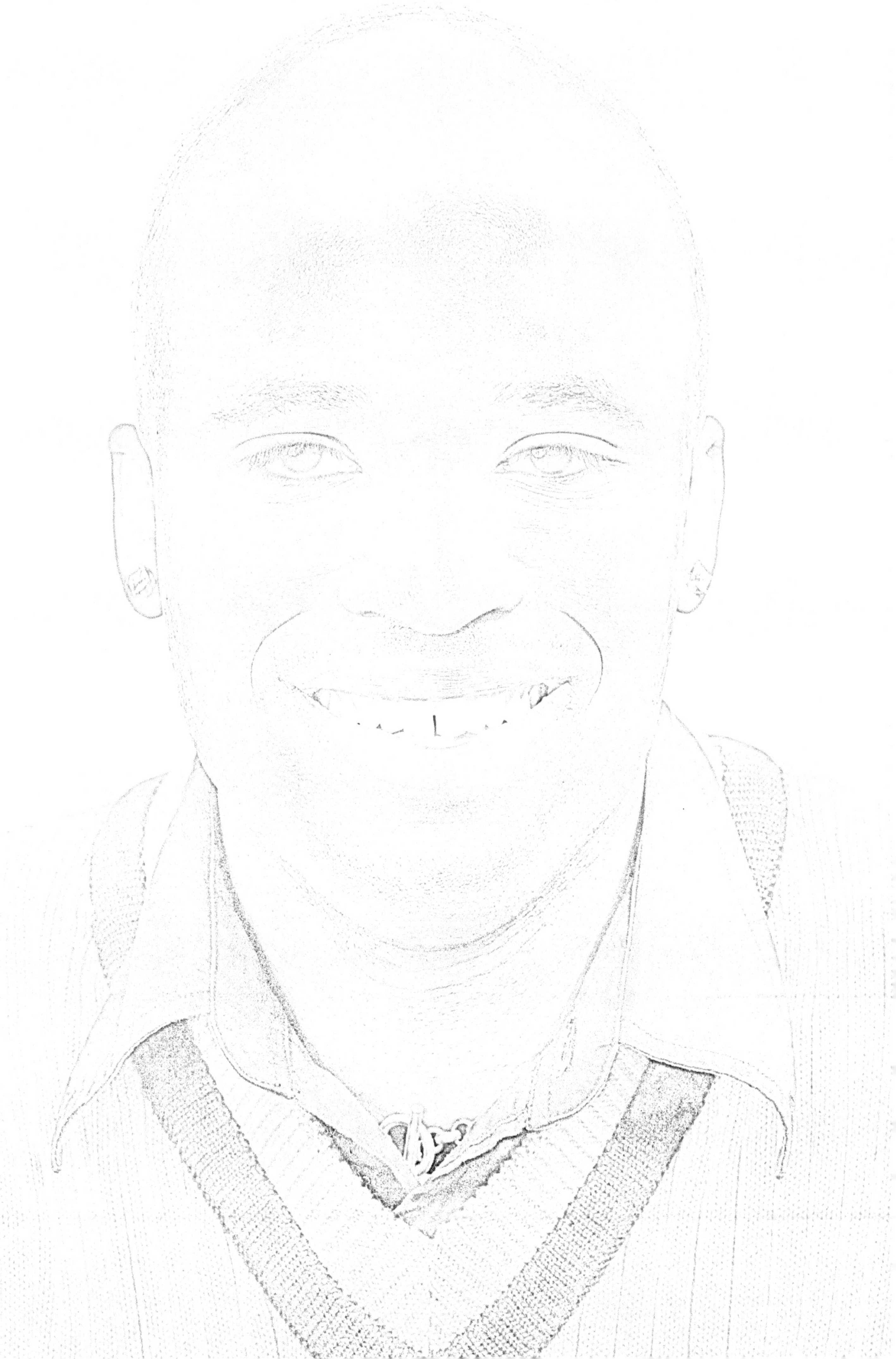

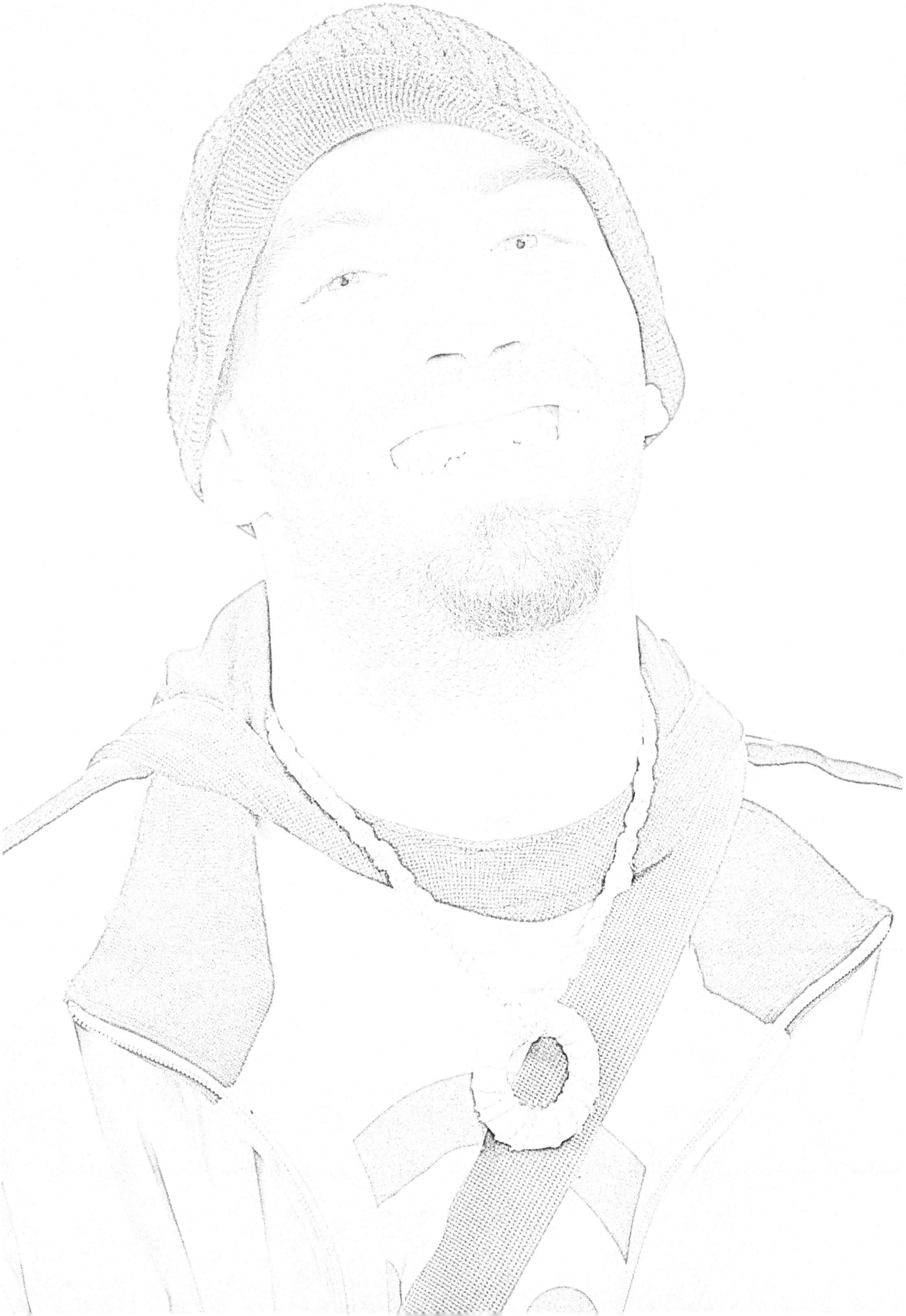

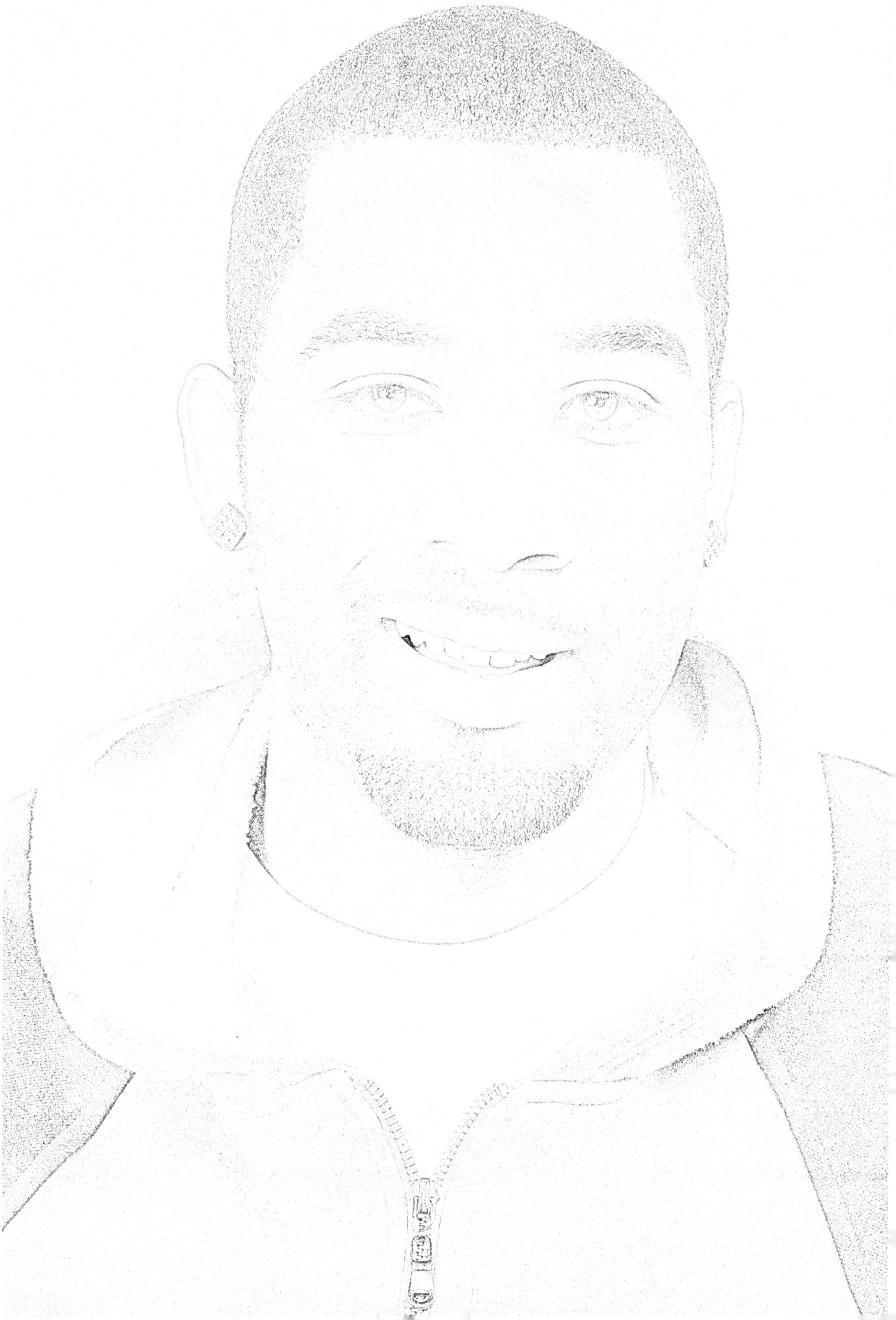

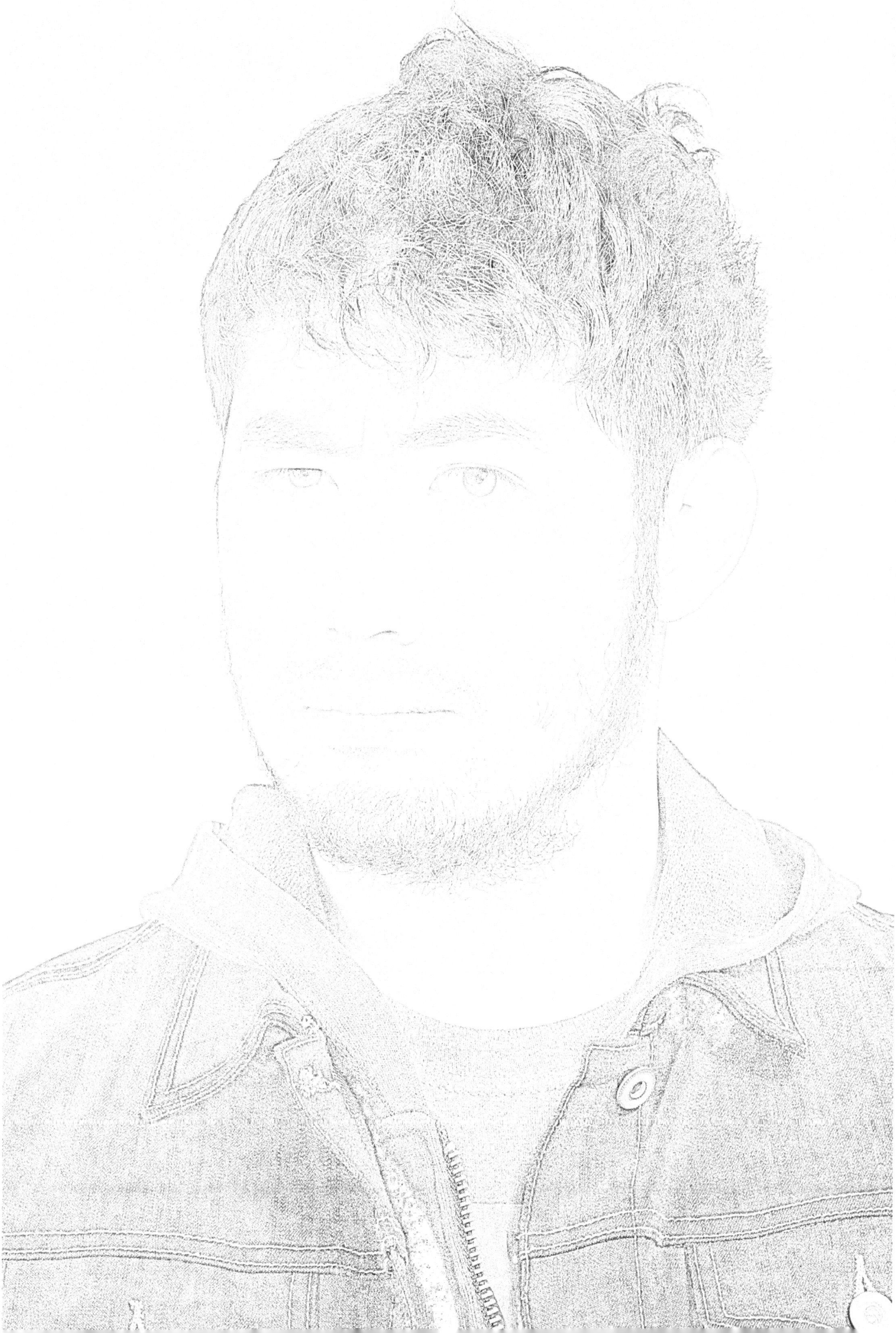

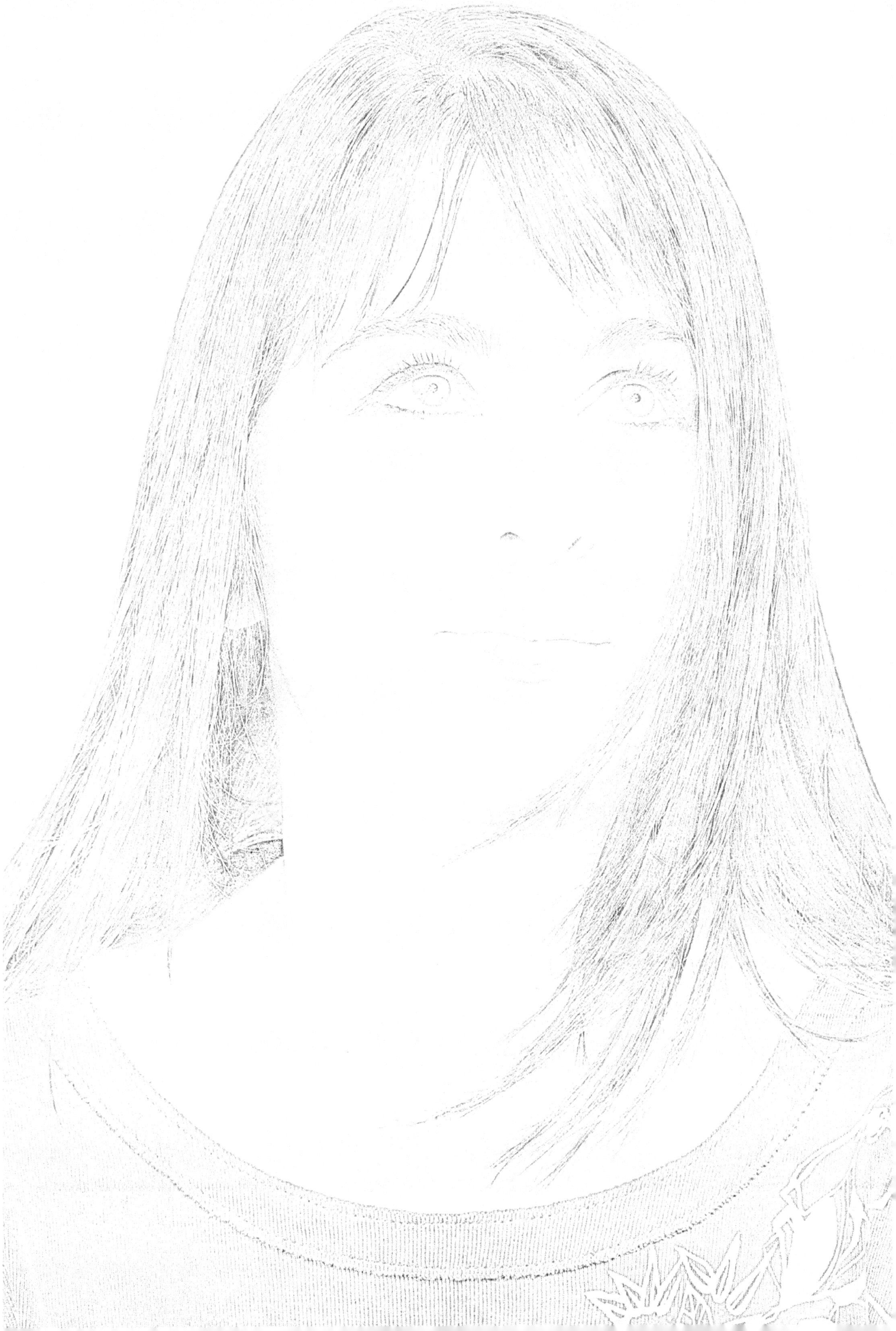

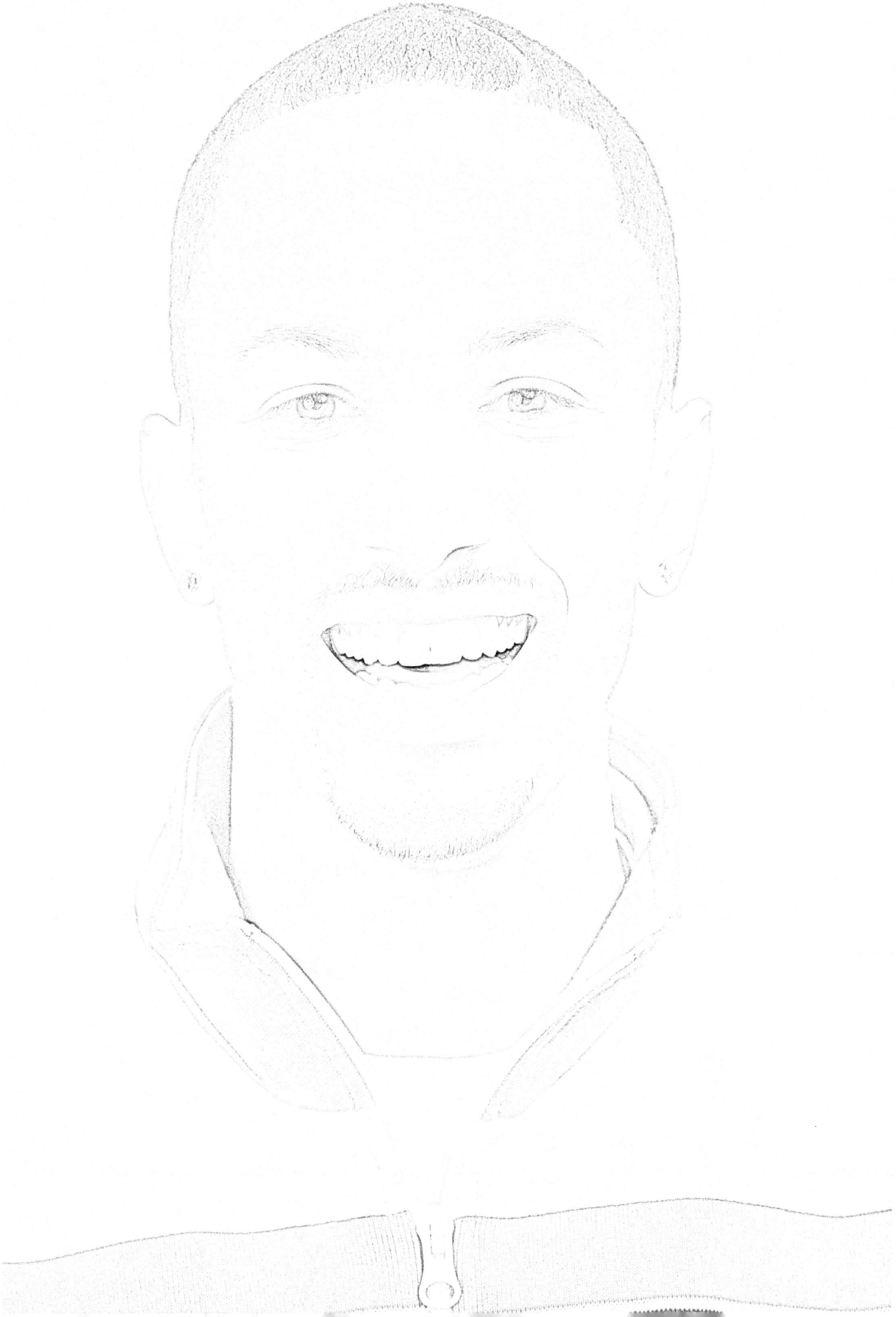

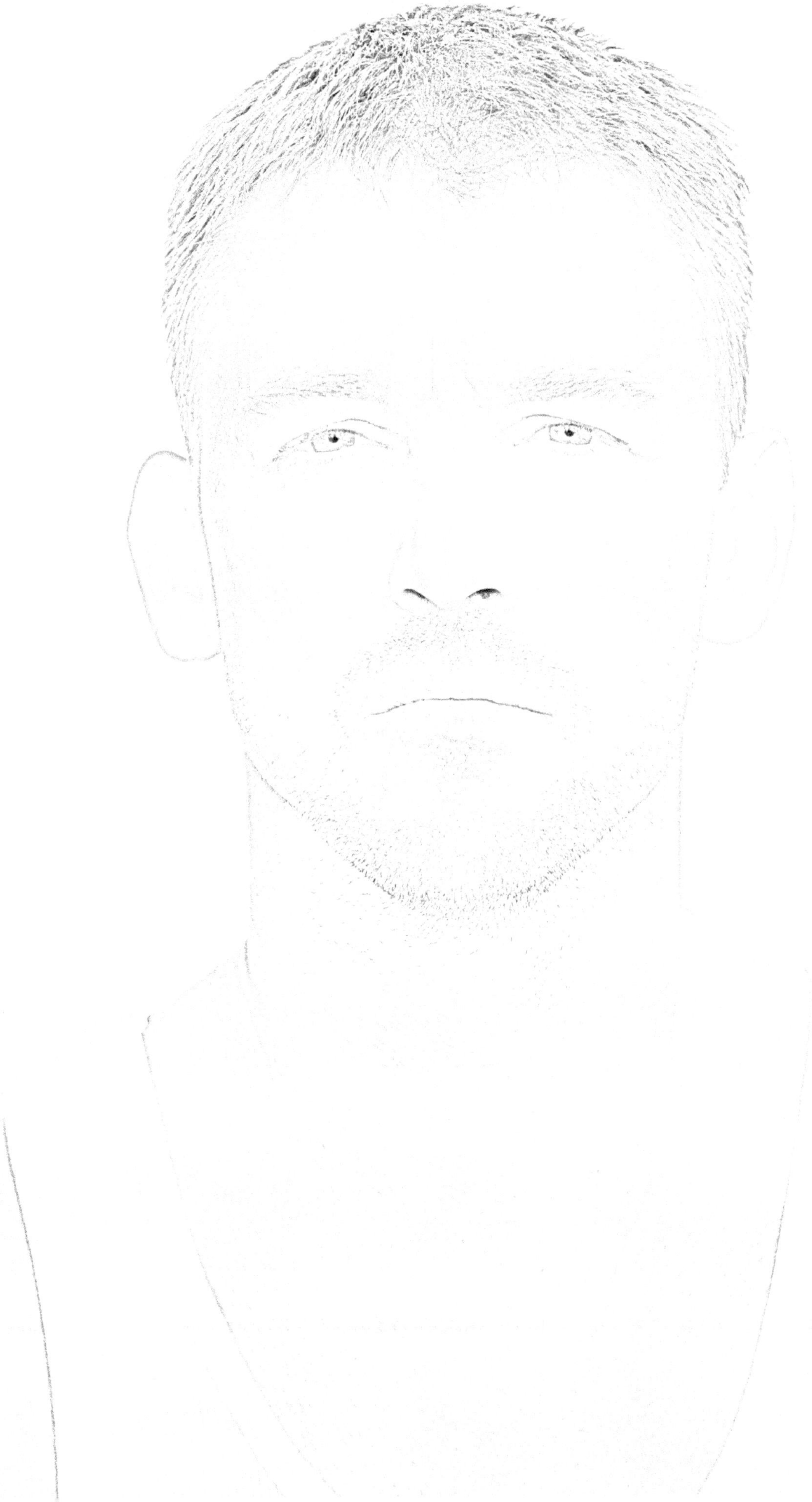

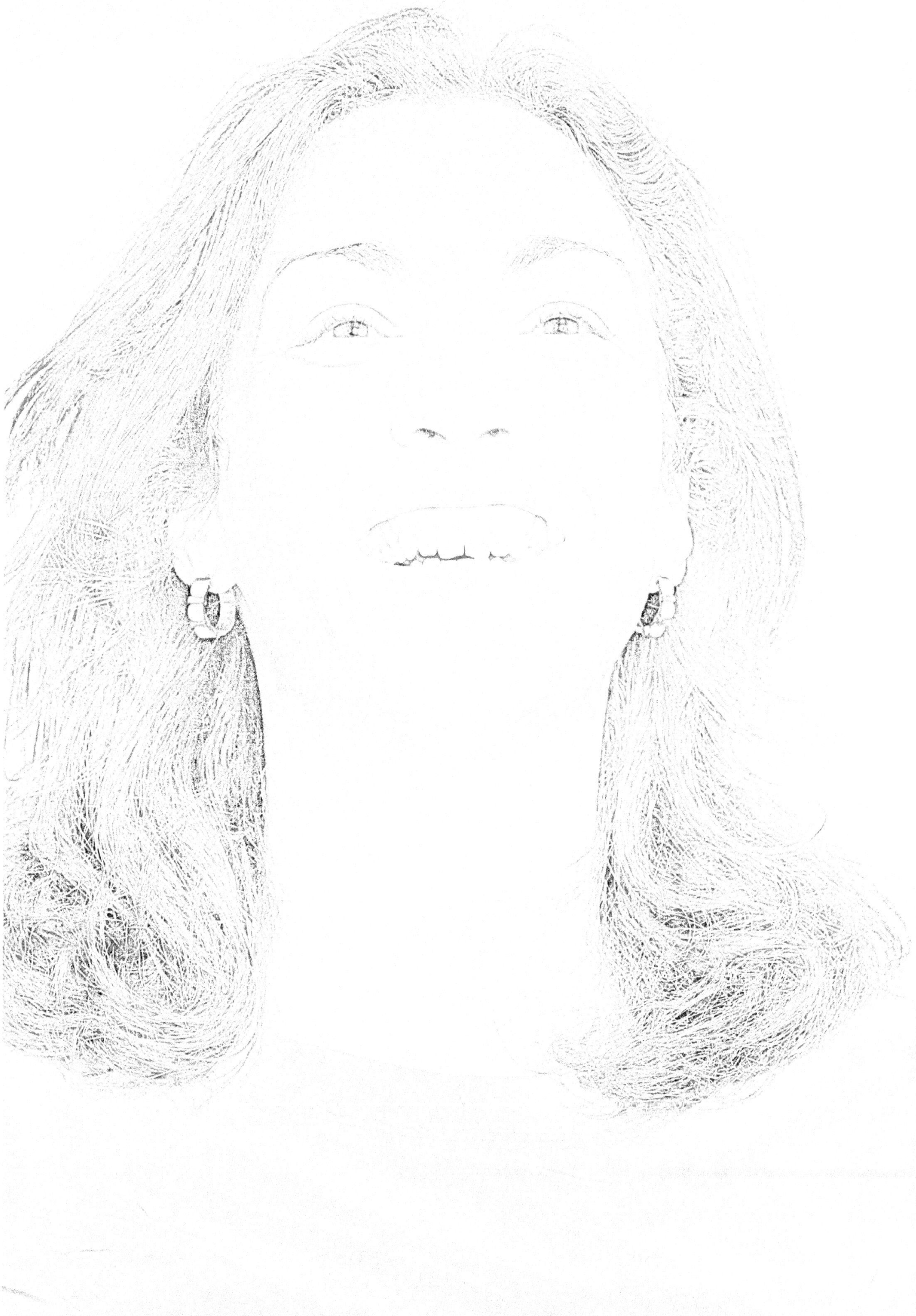

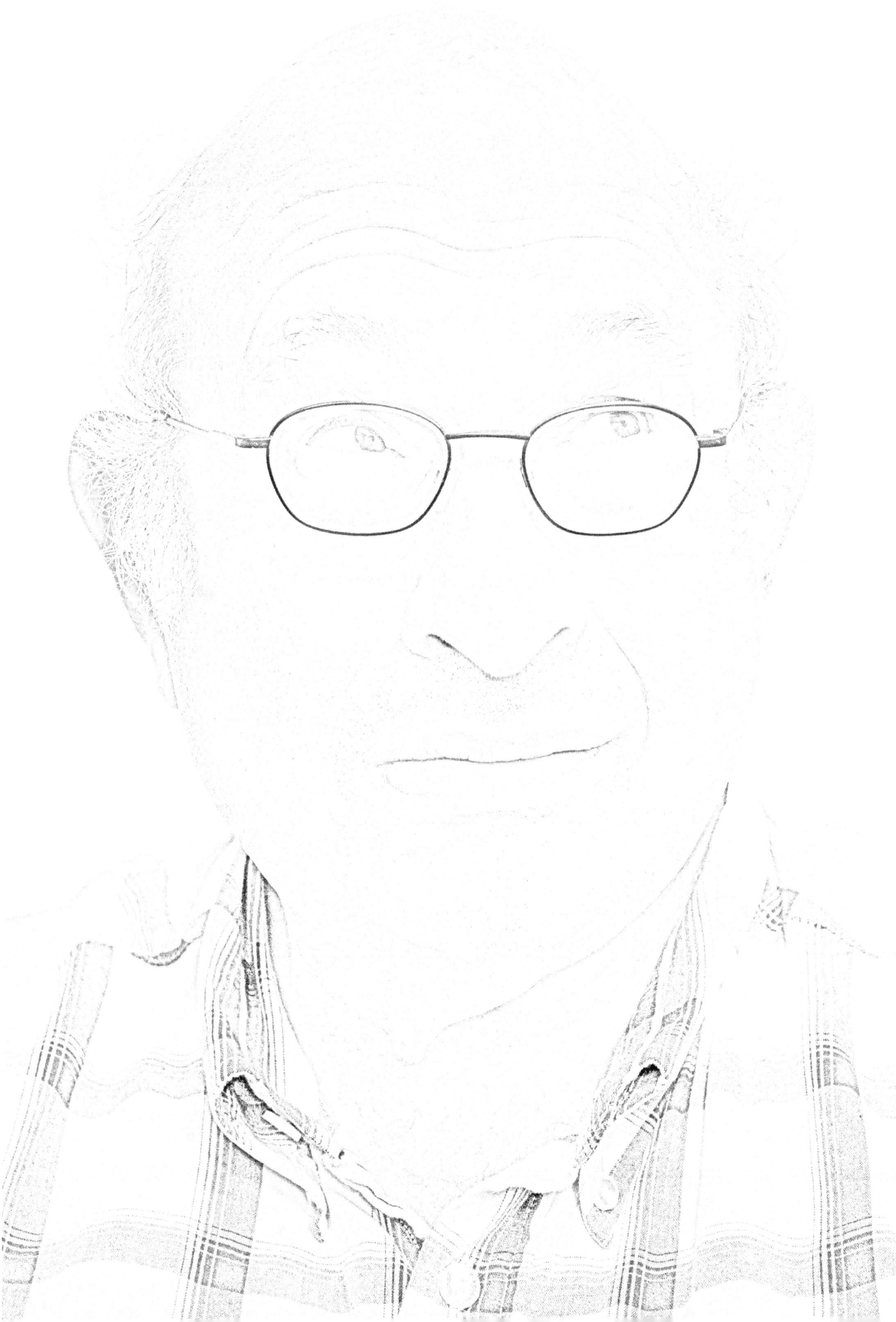

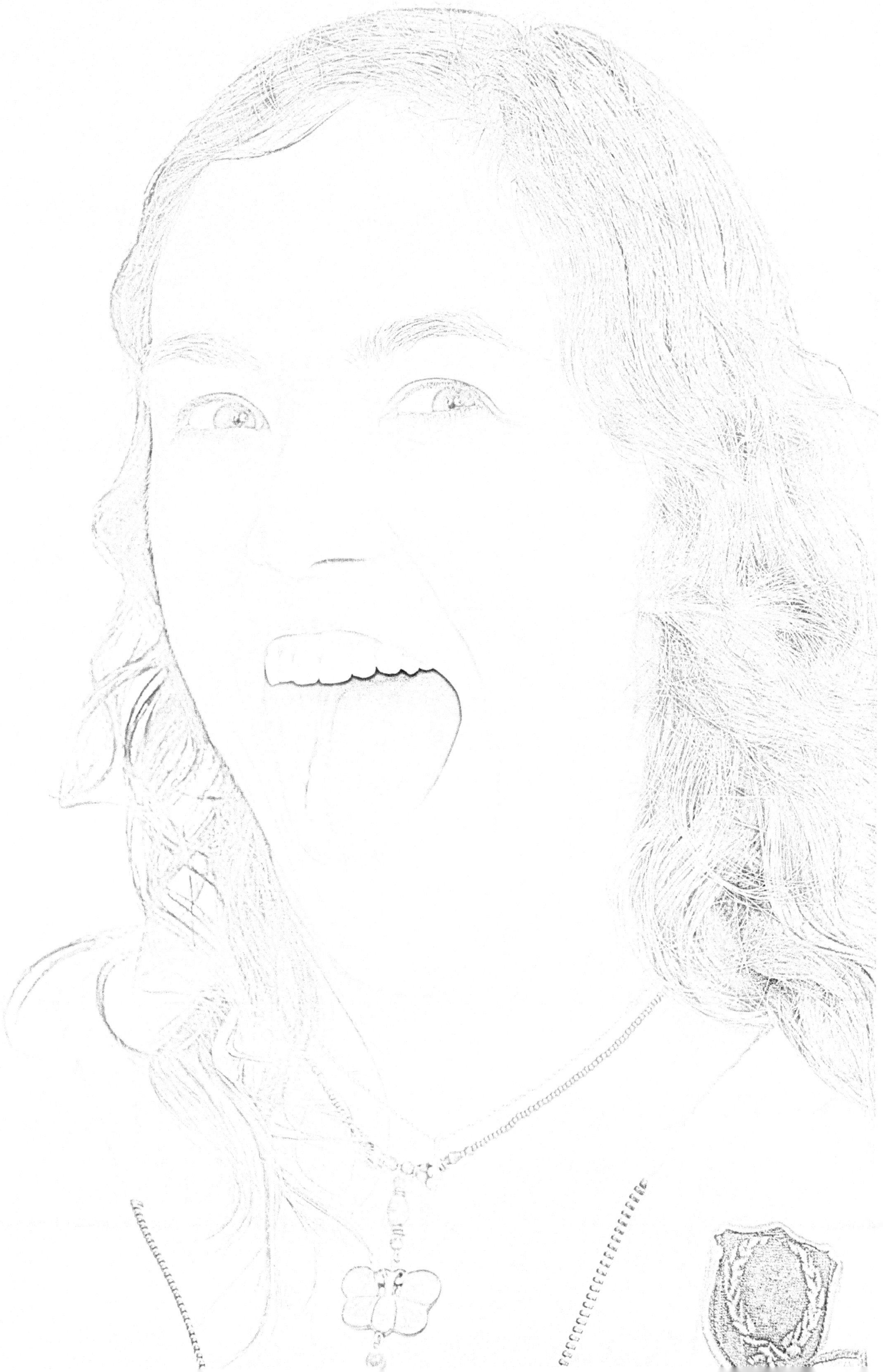

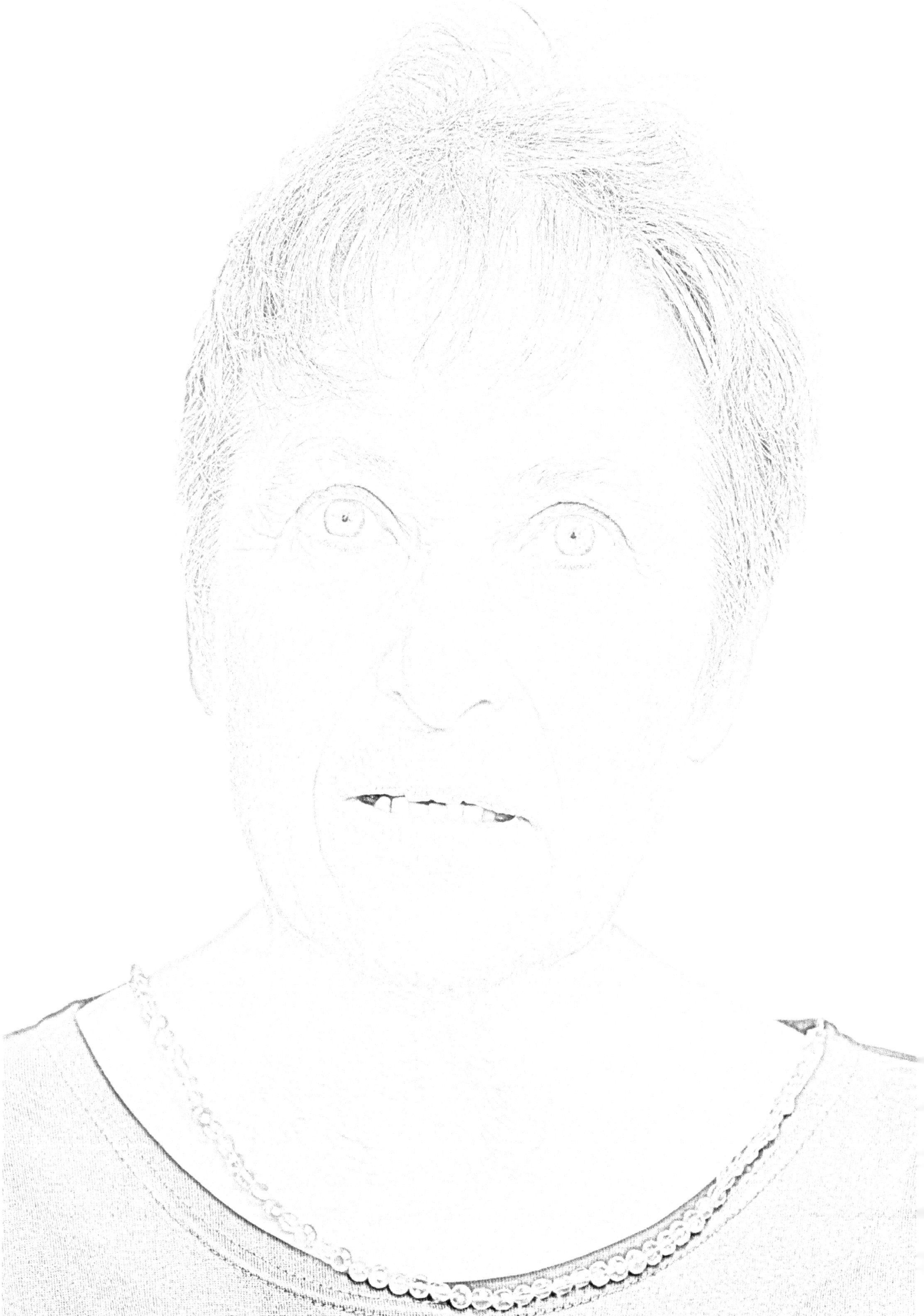

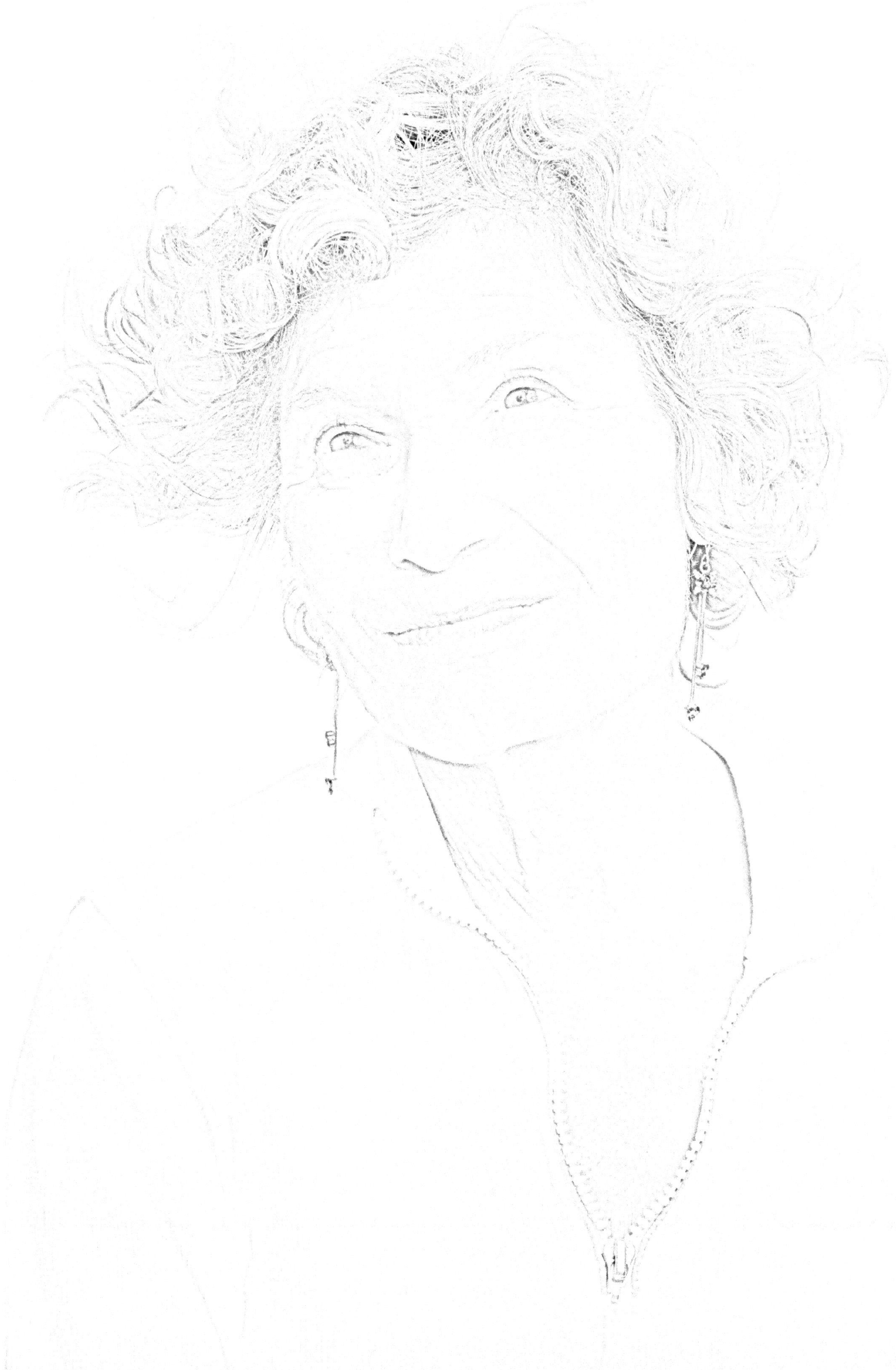

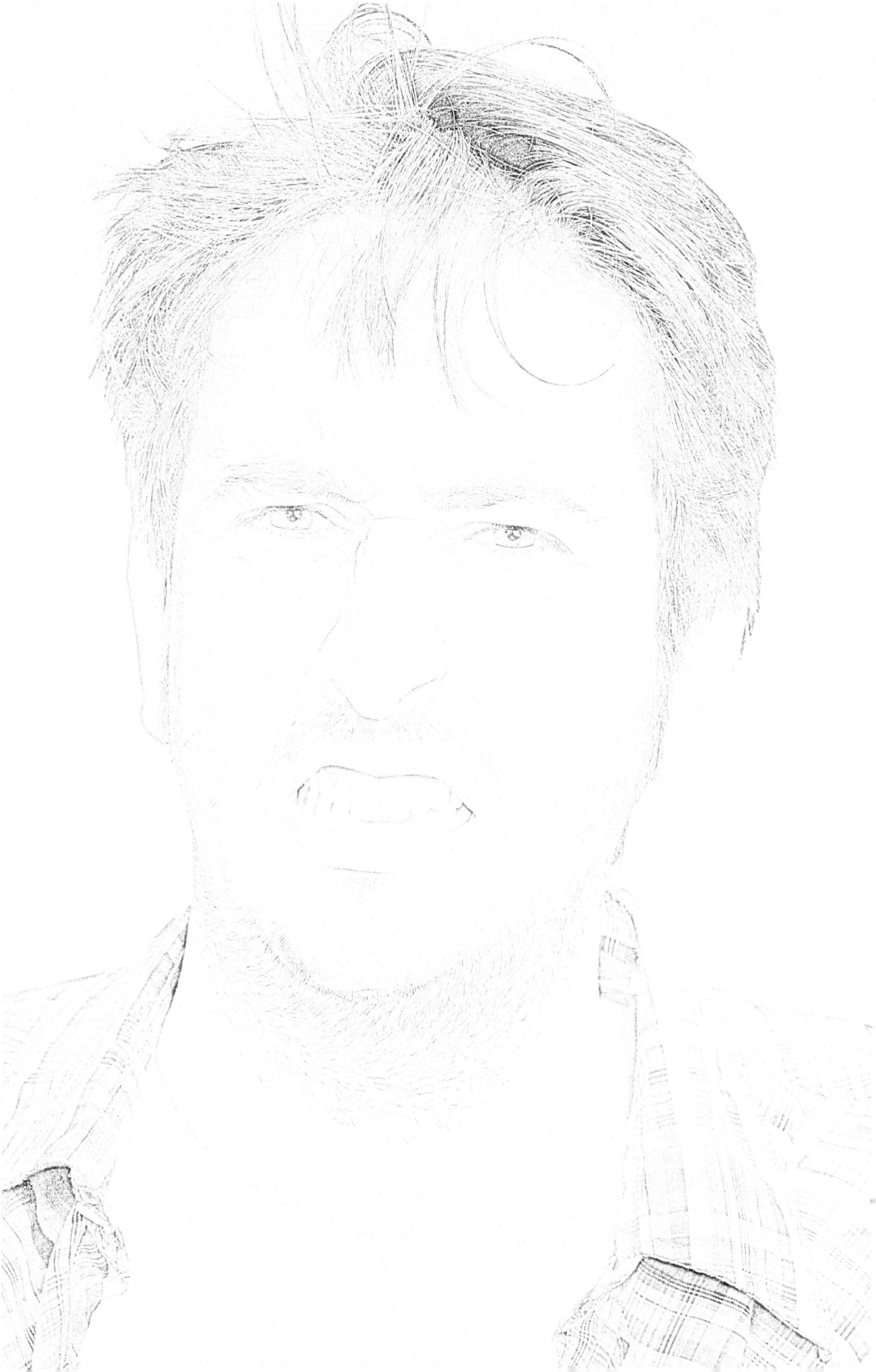

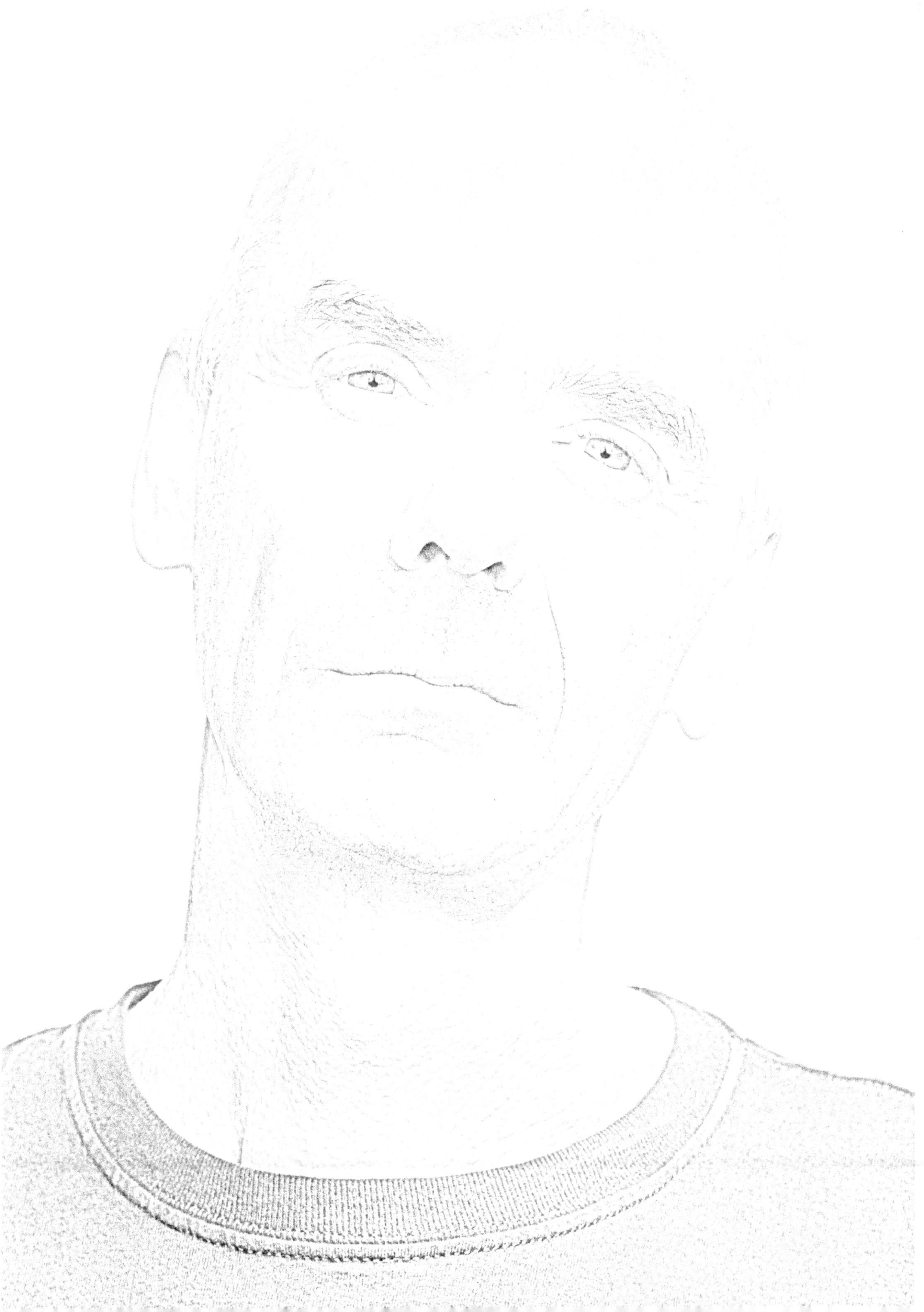

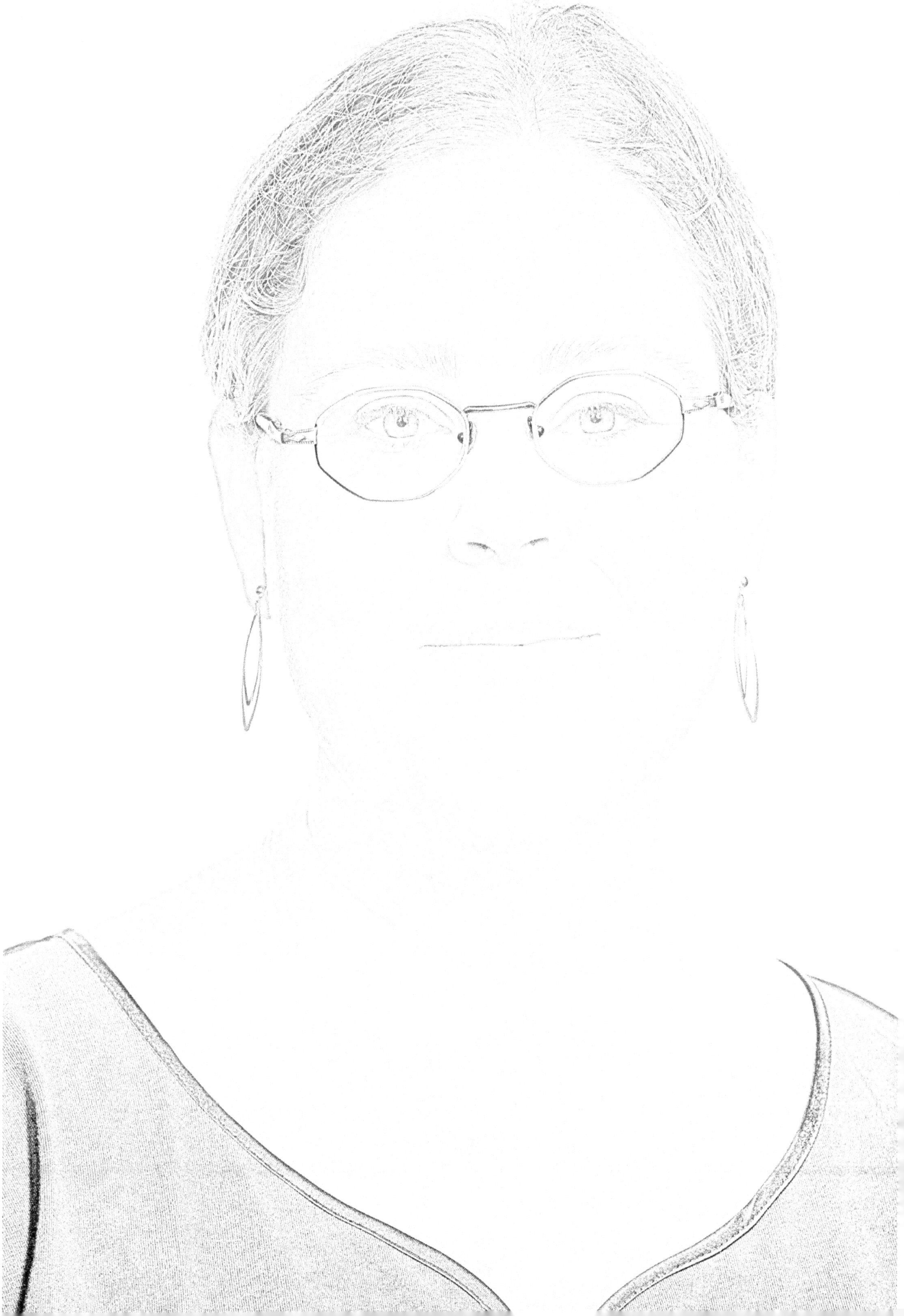

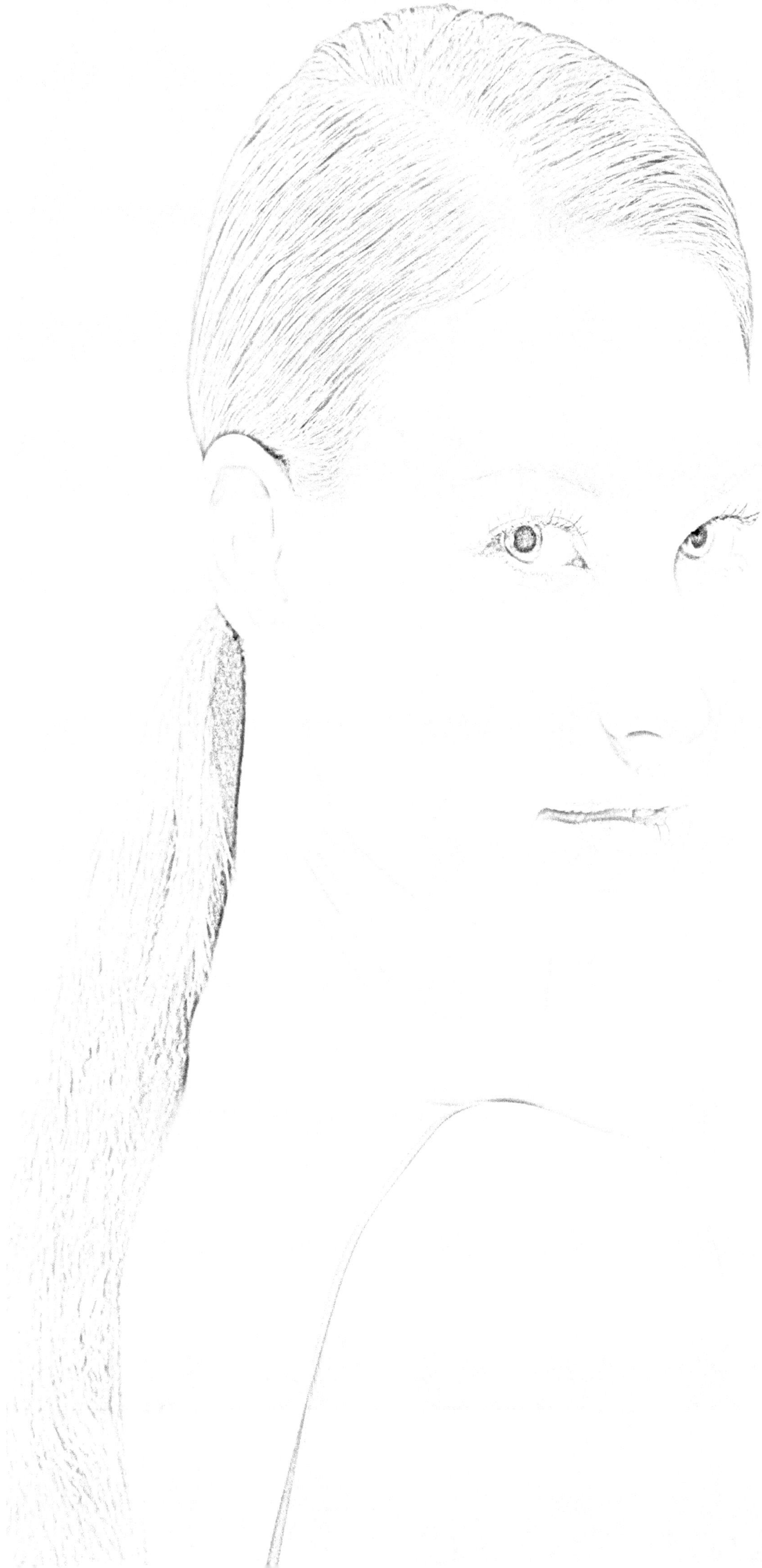

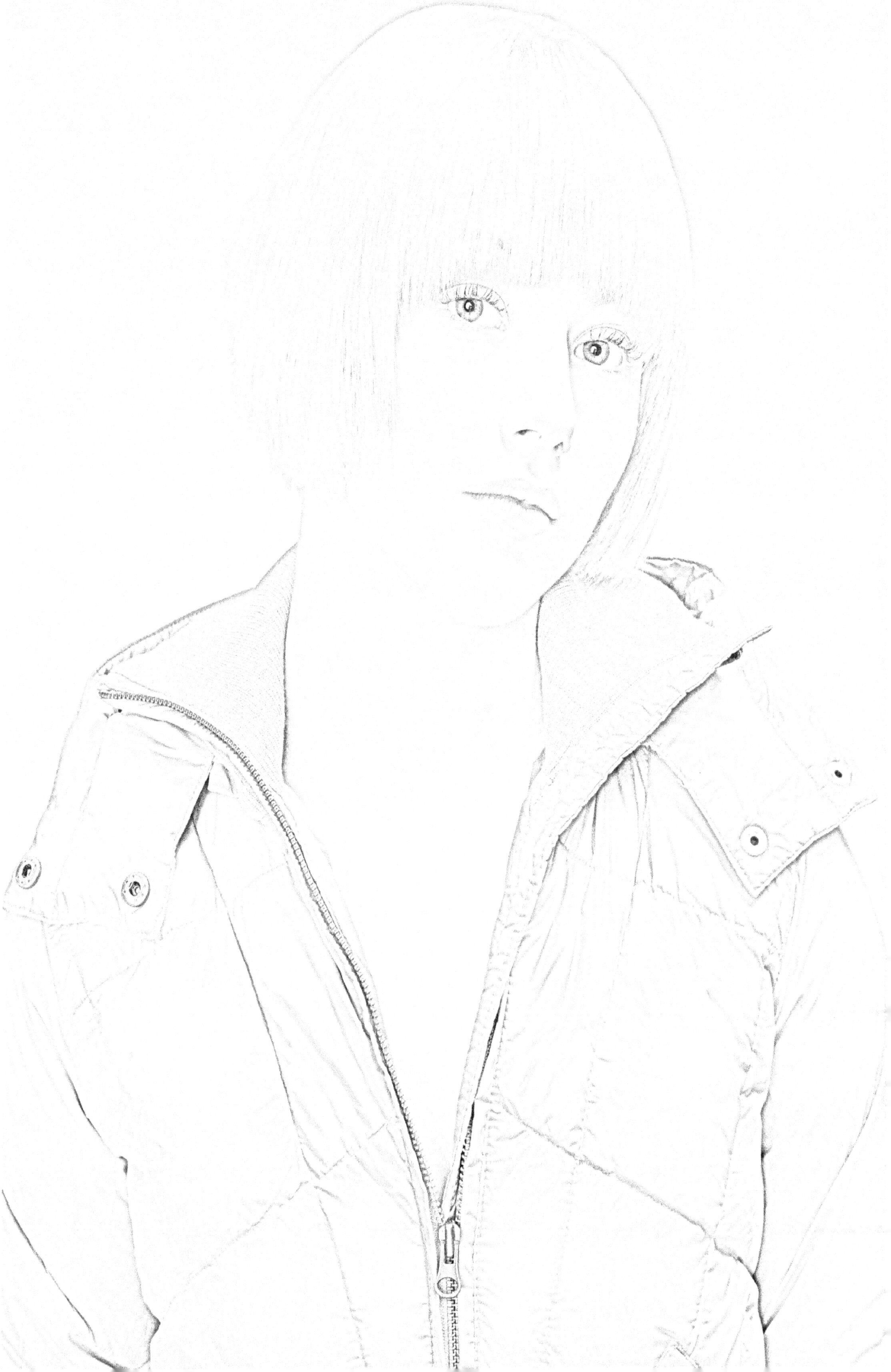

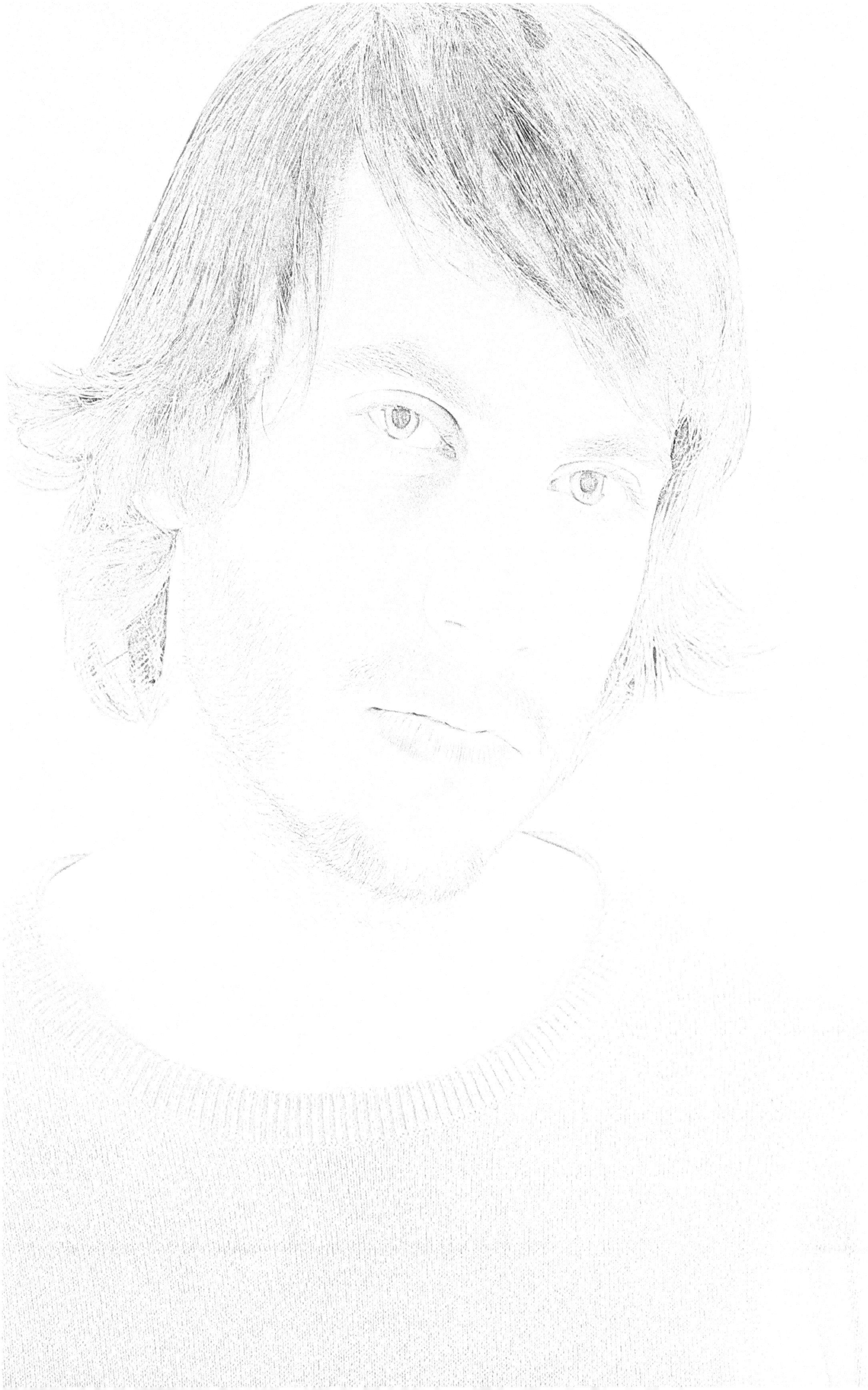

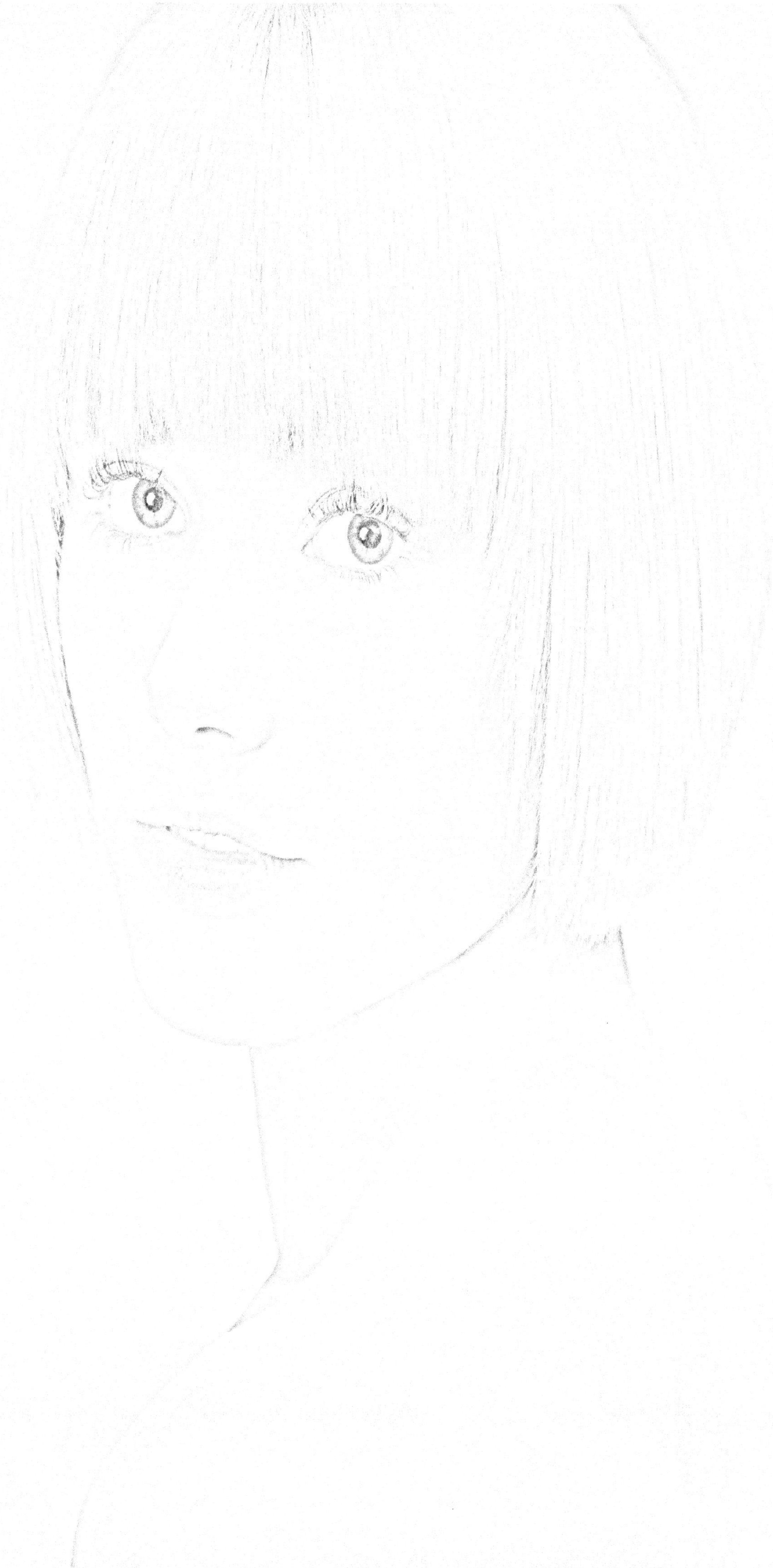

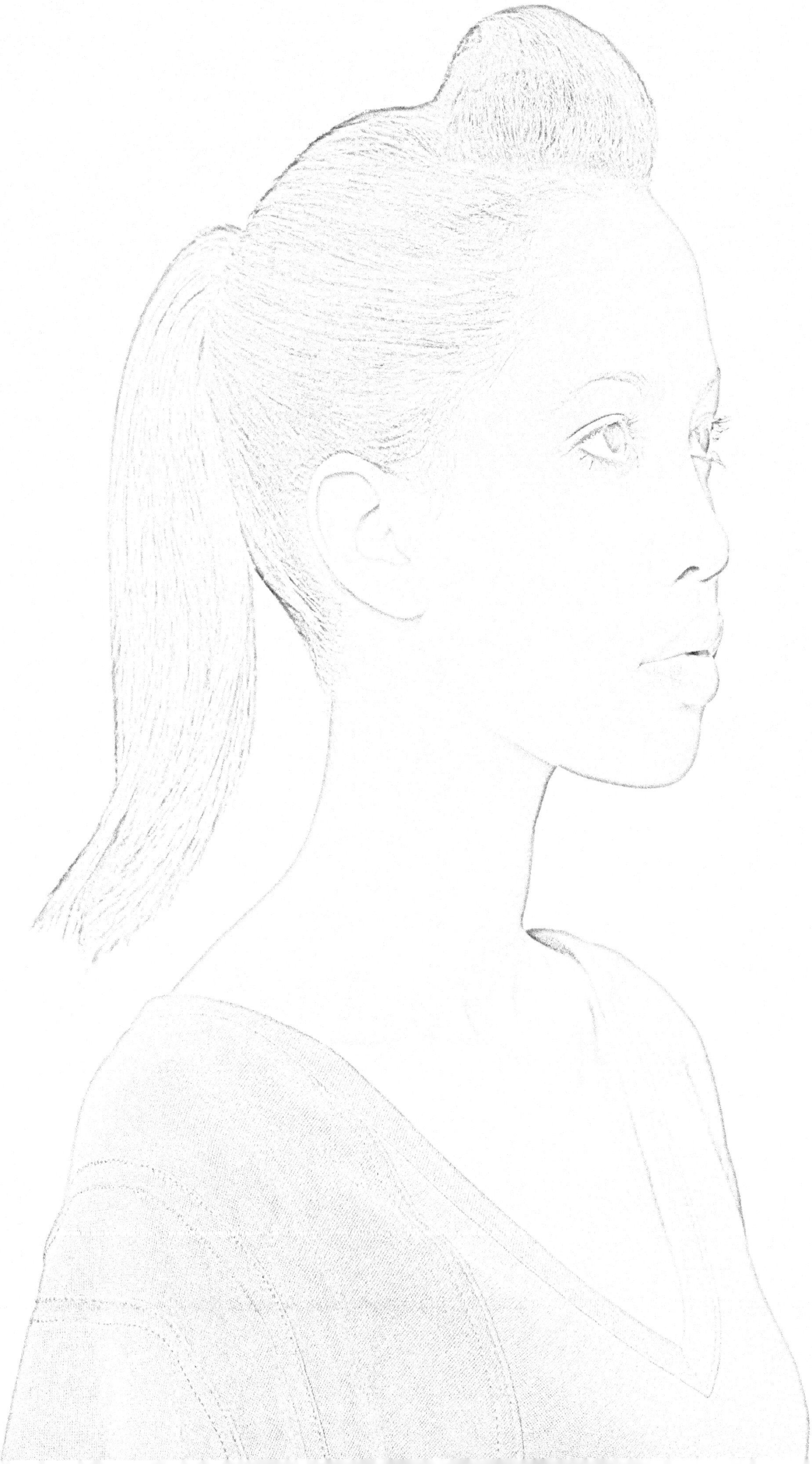

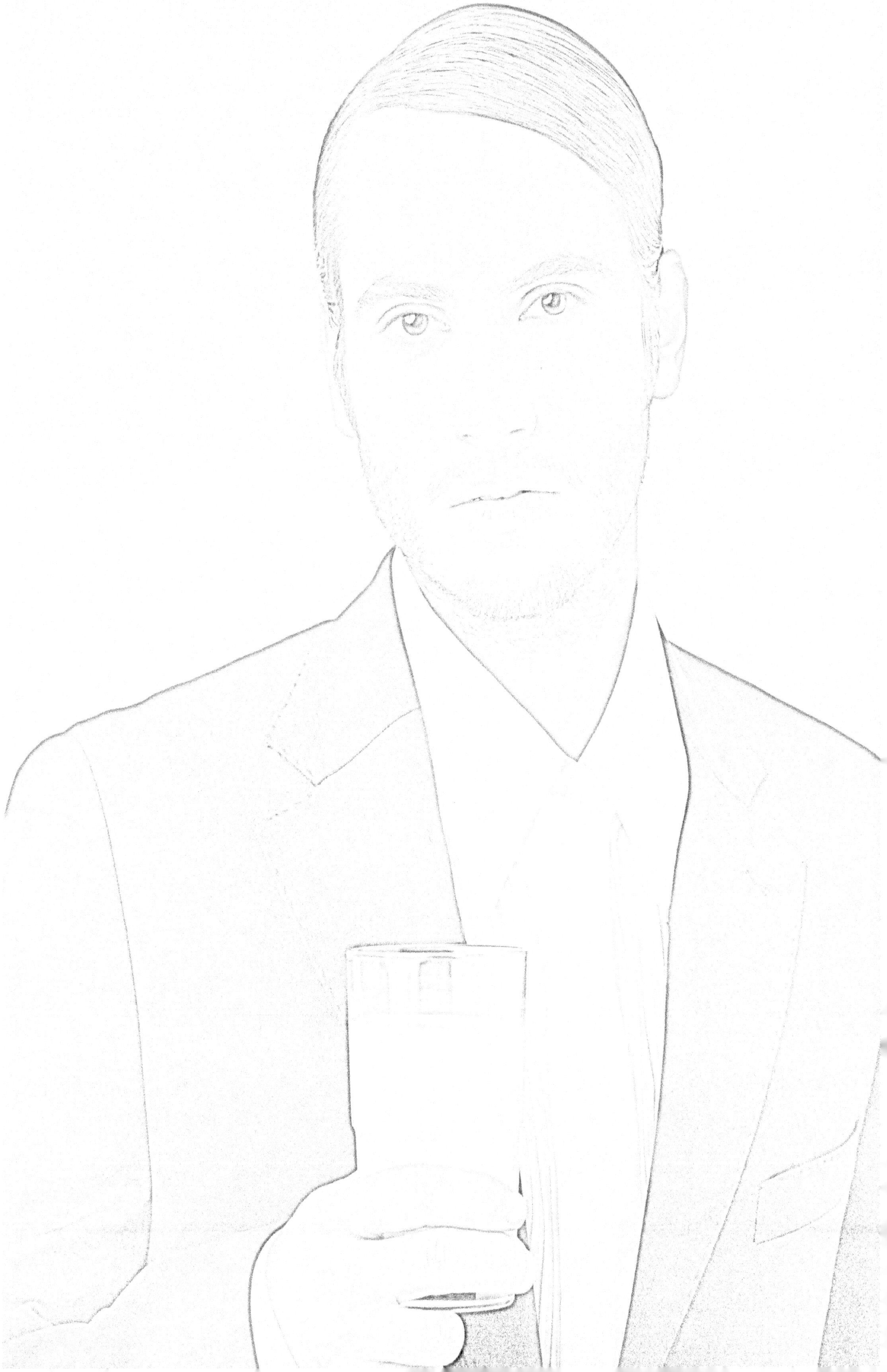

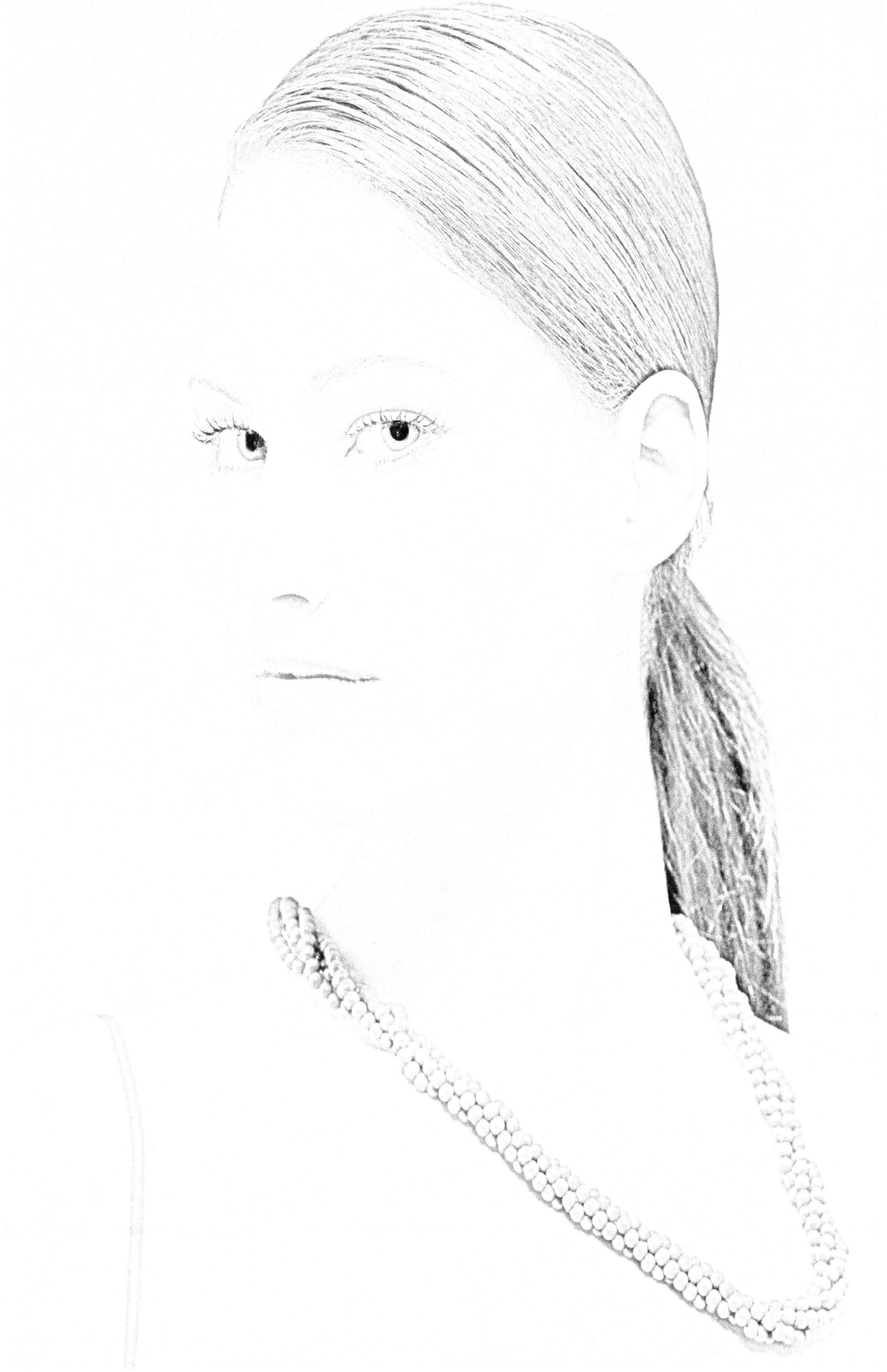

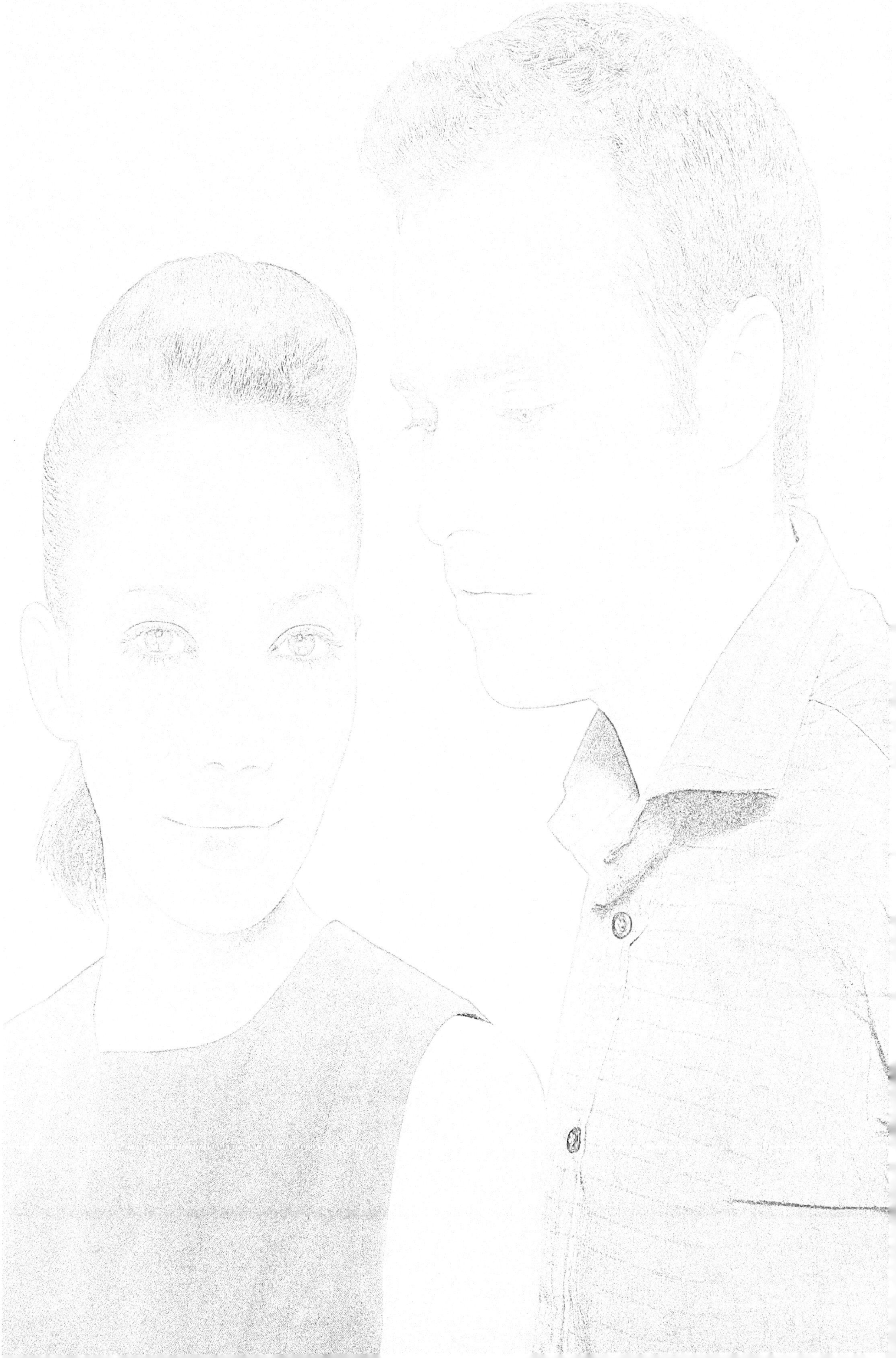

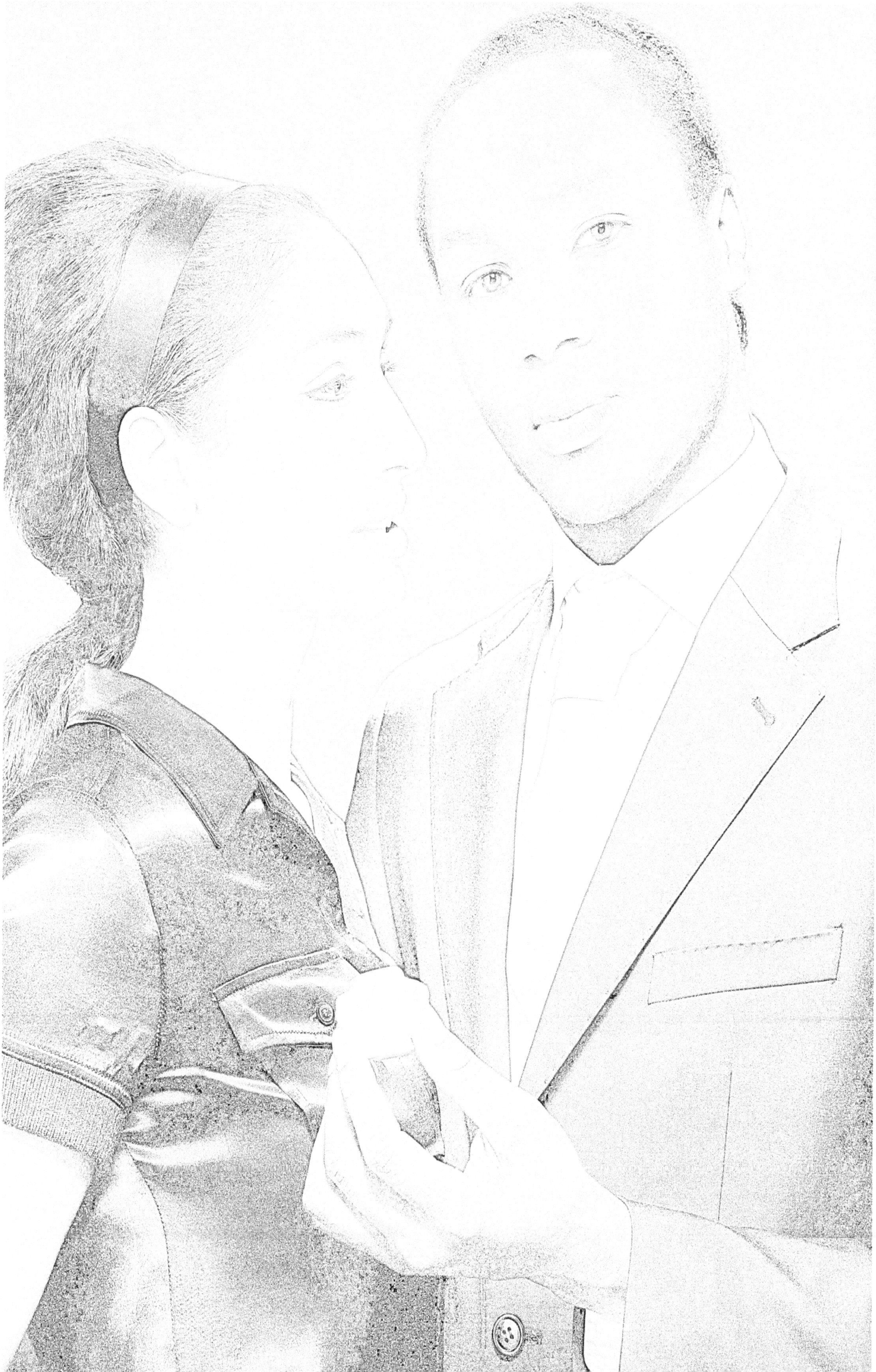

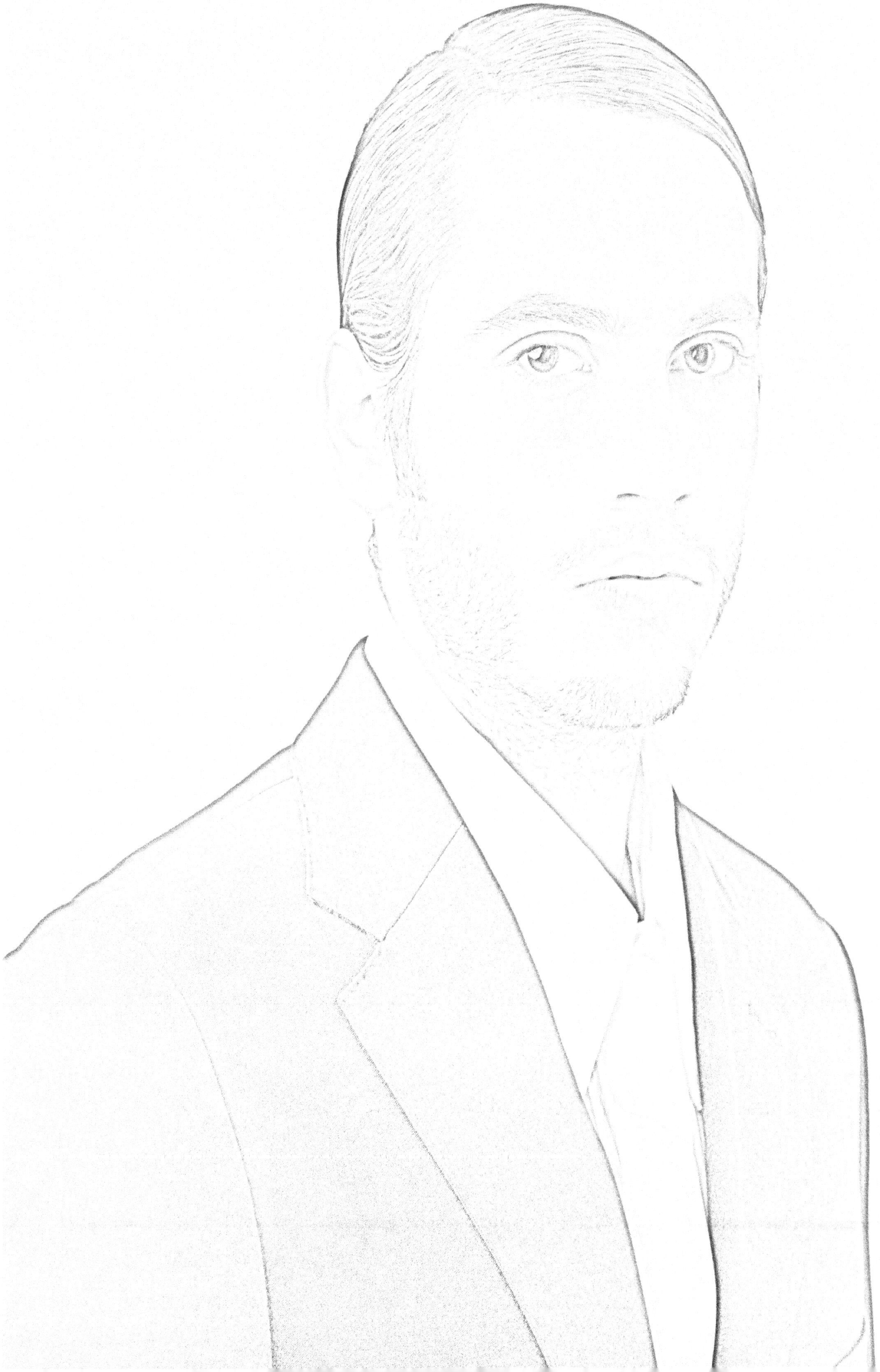

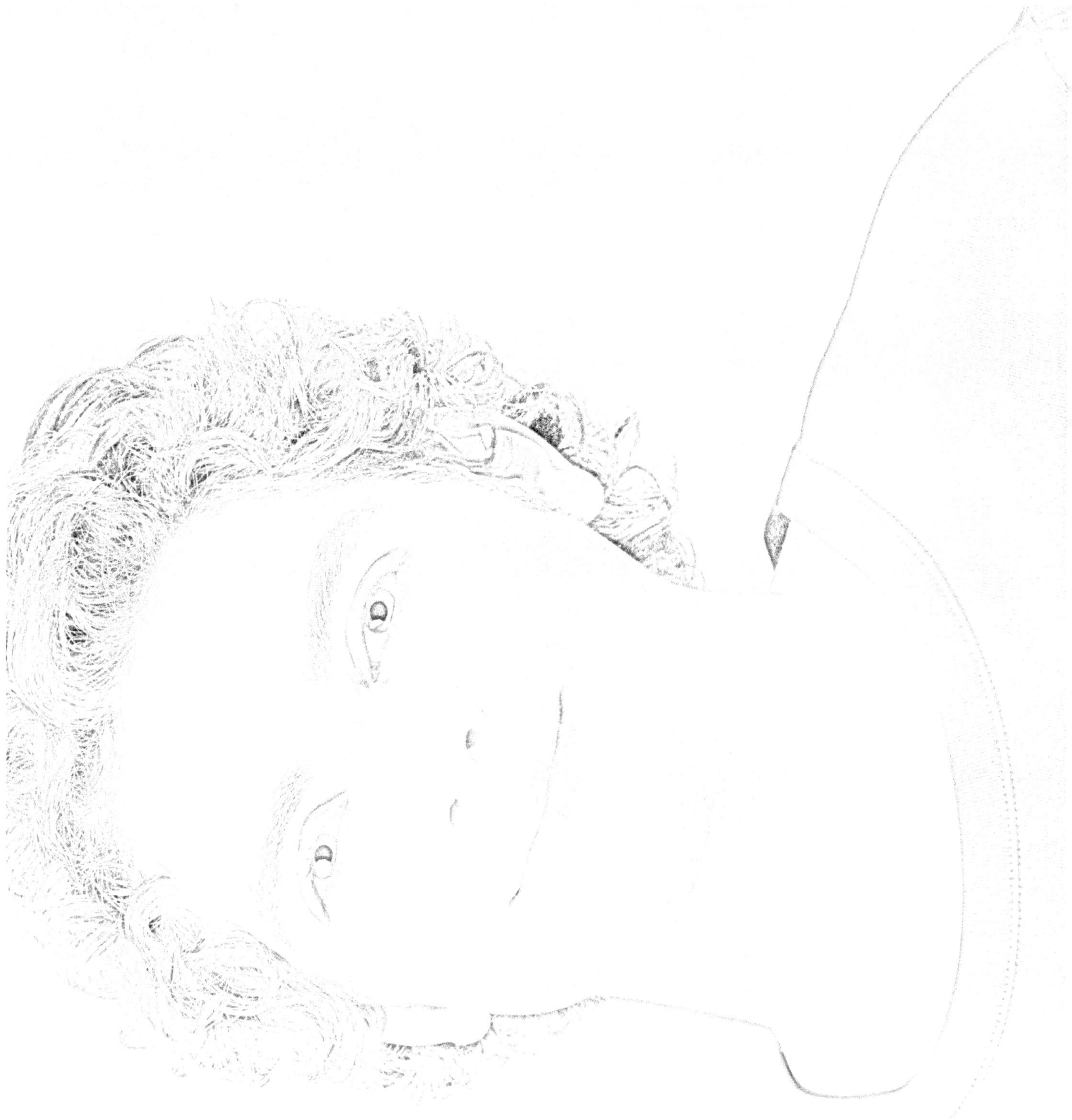

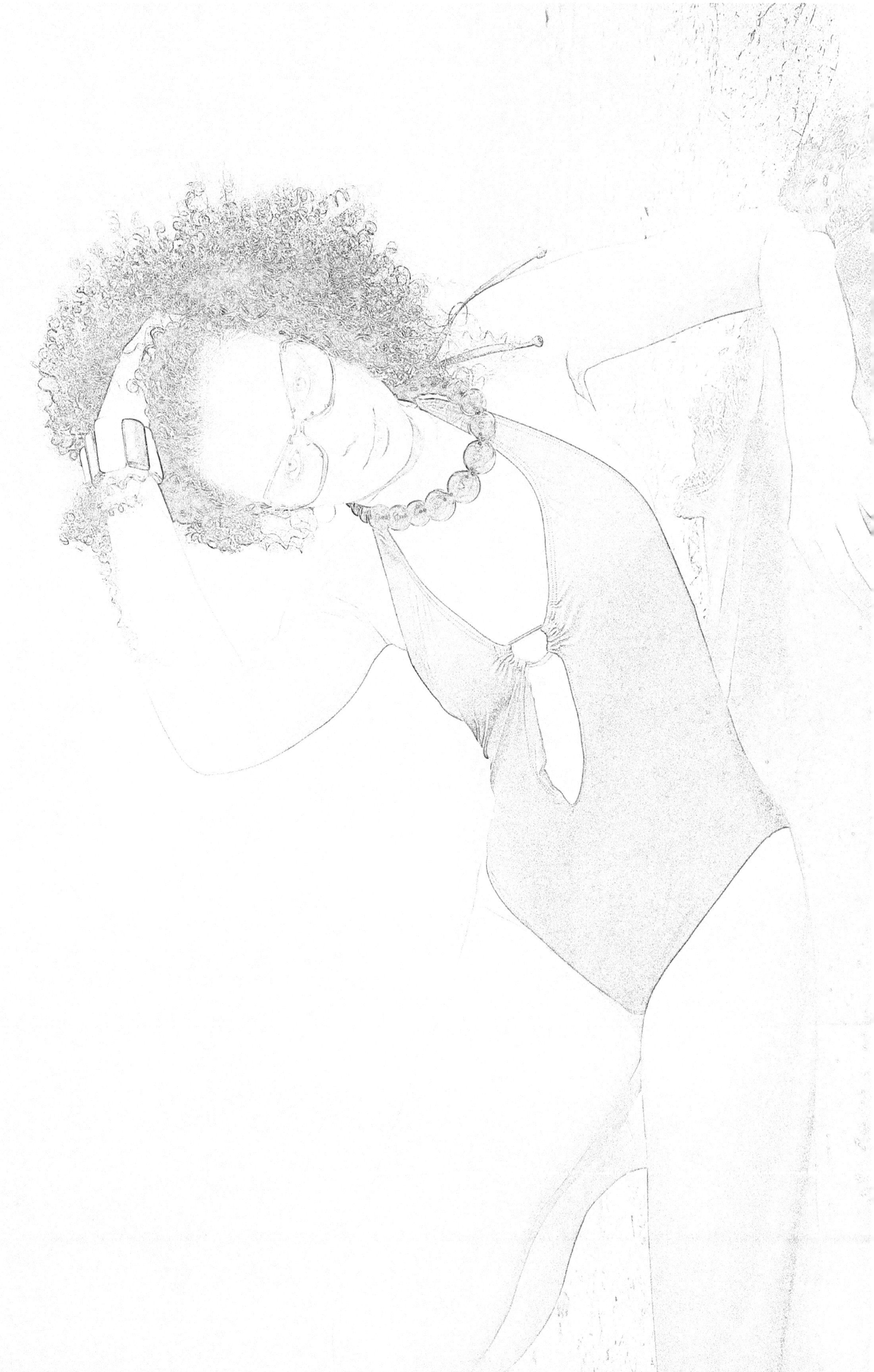

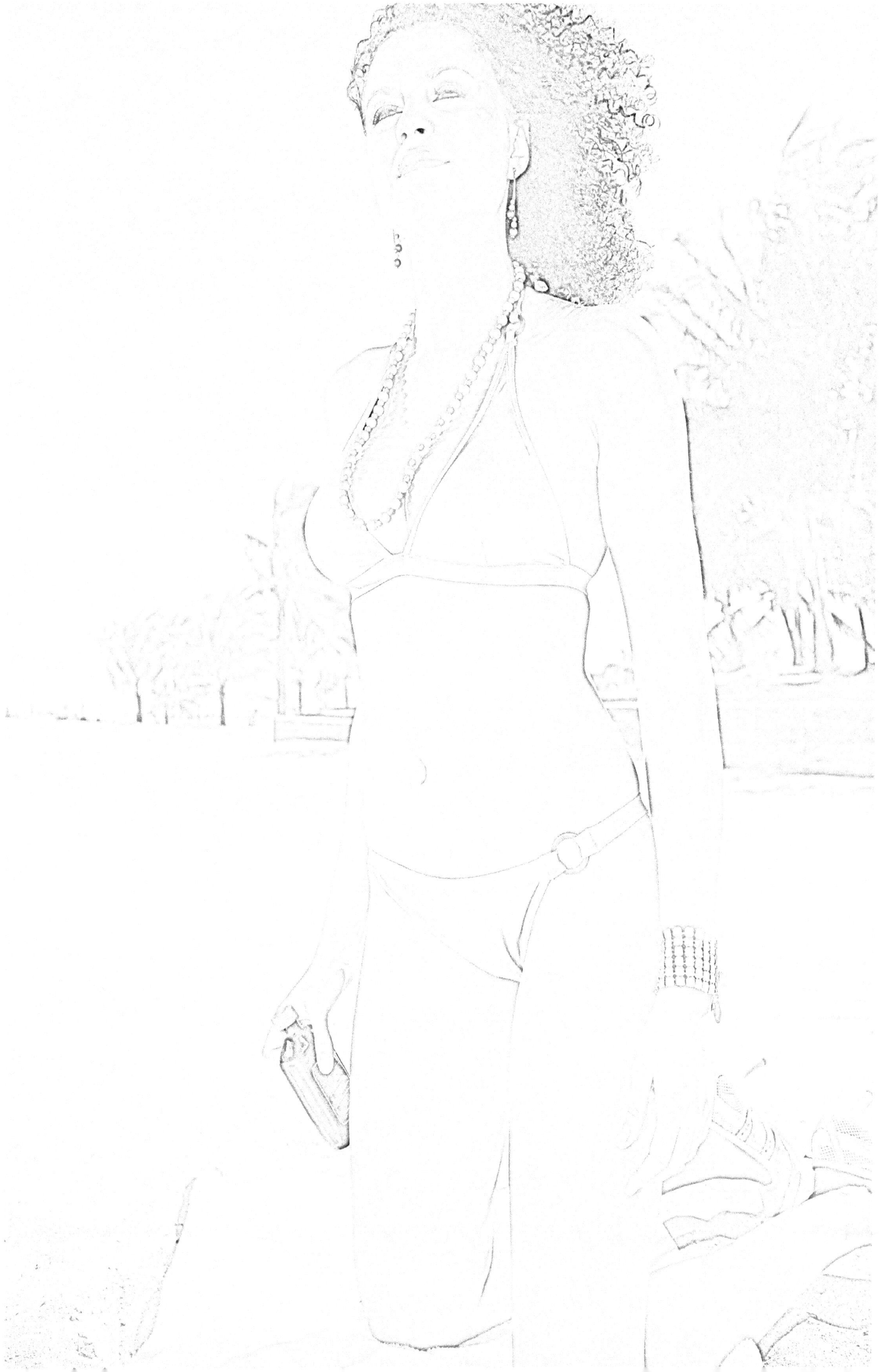

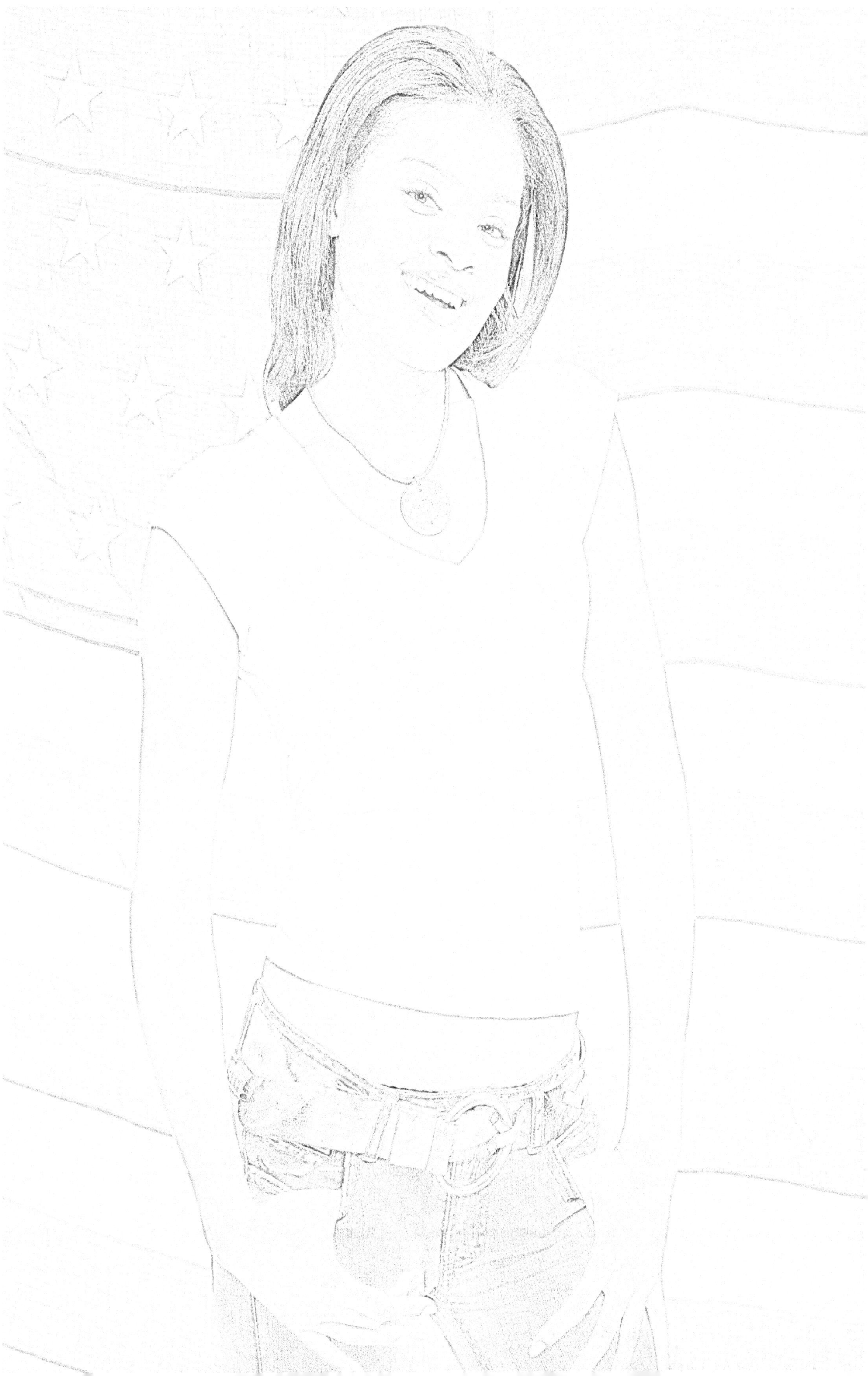

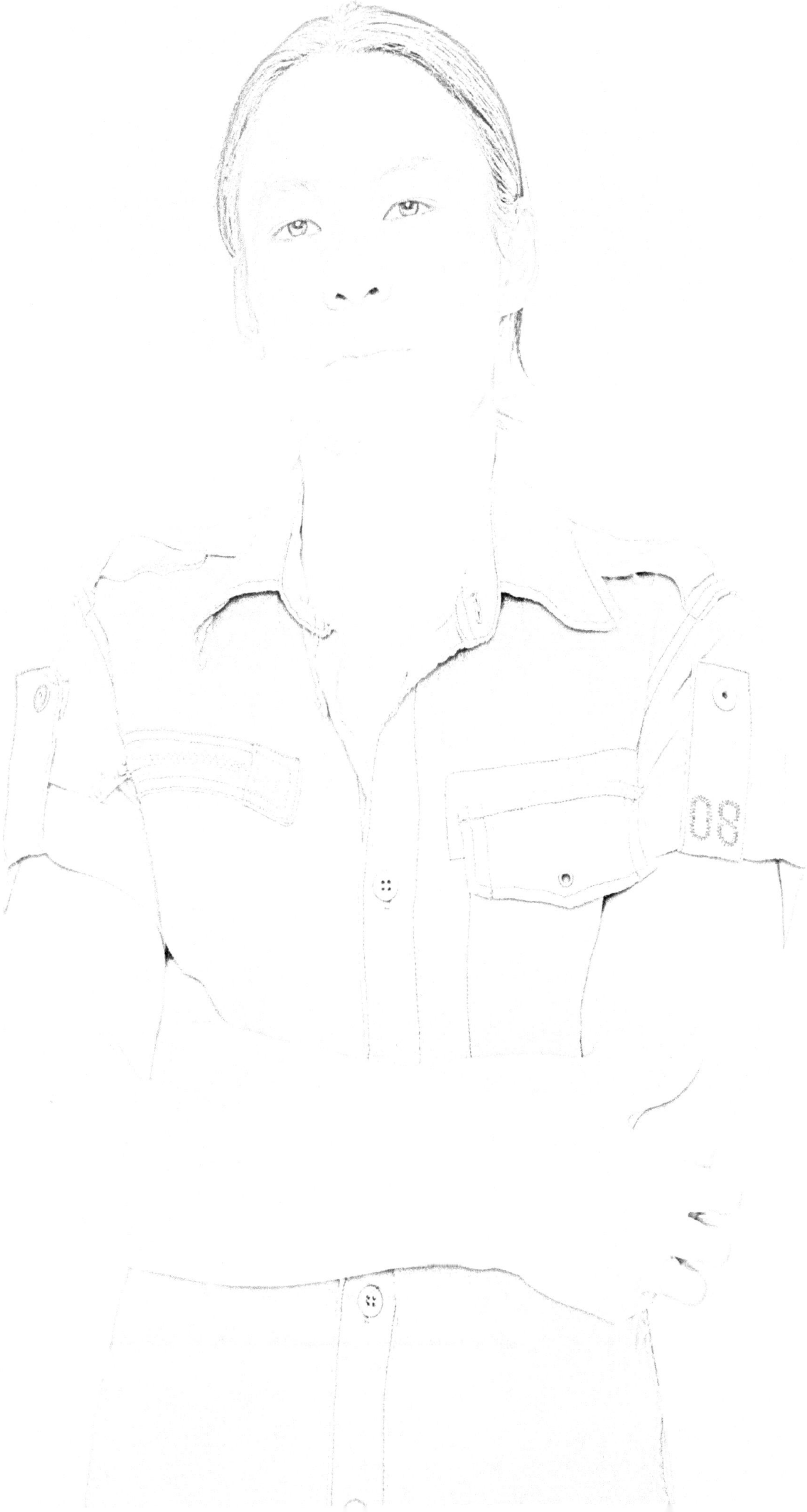
08

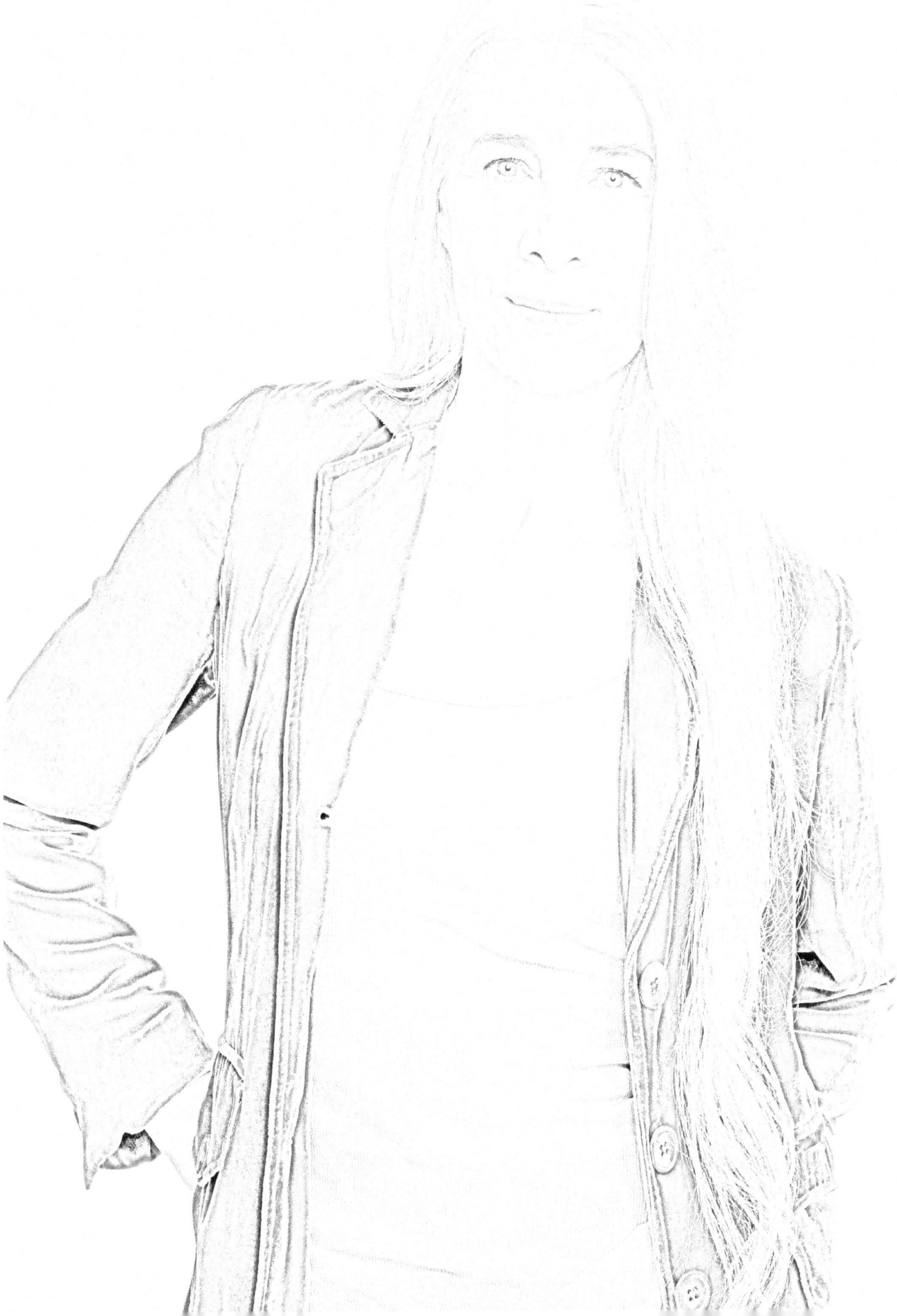

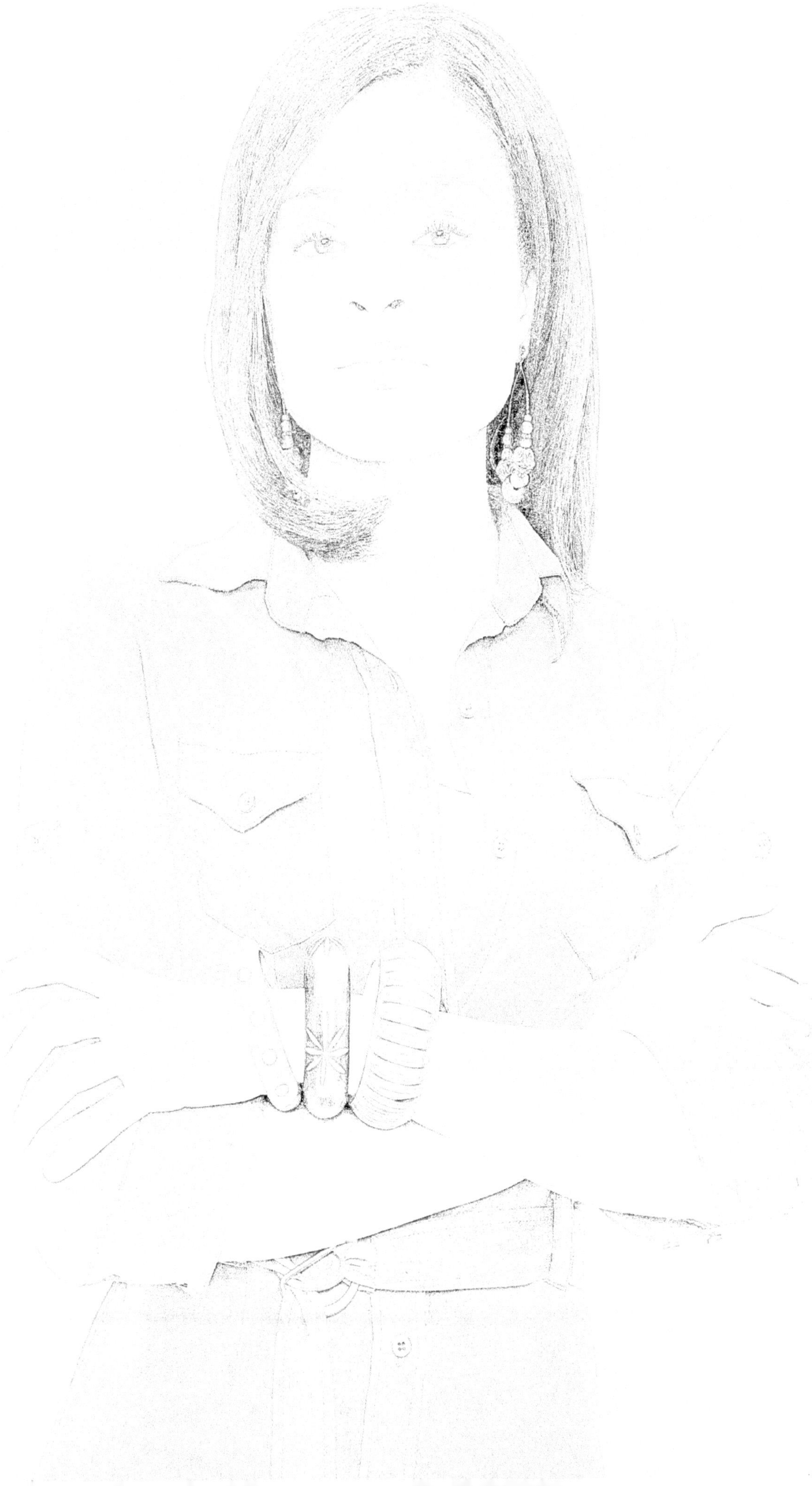

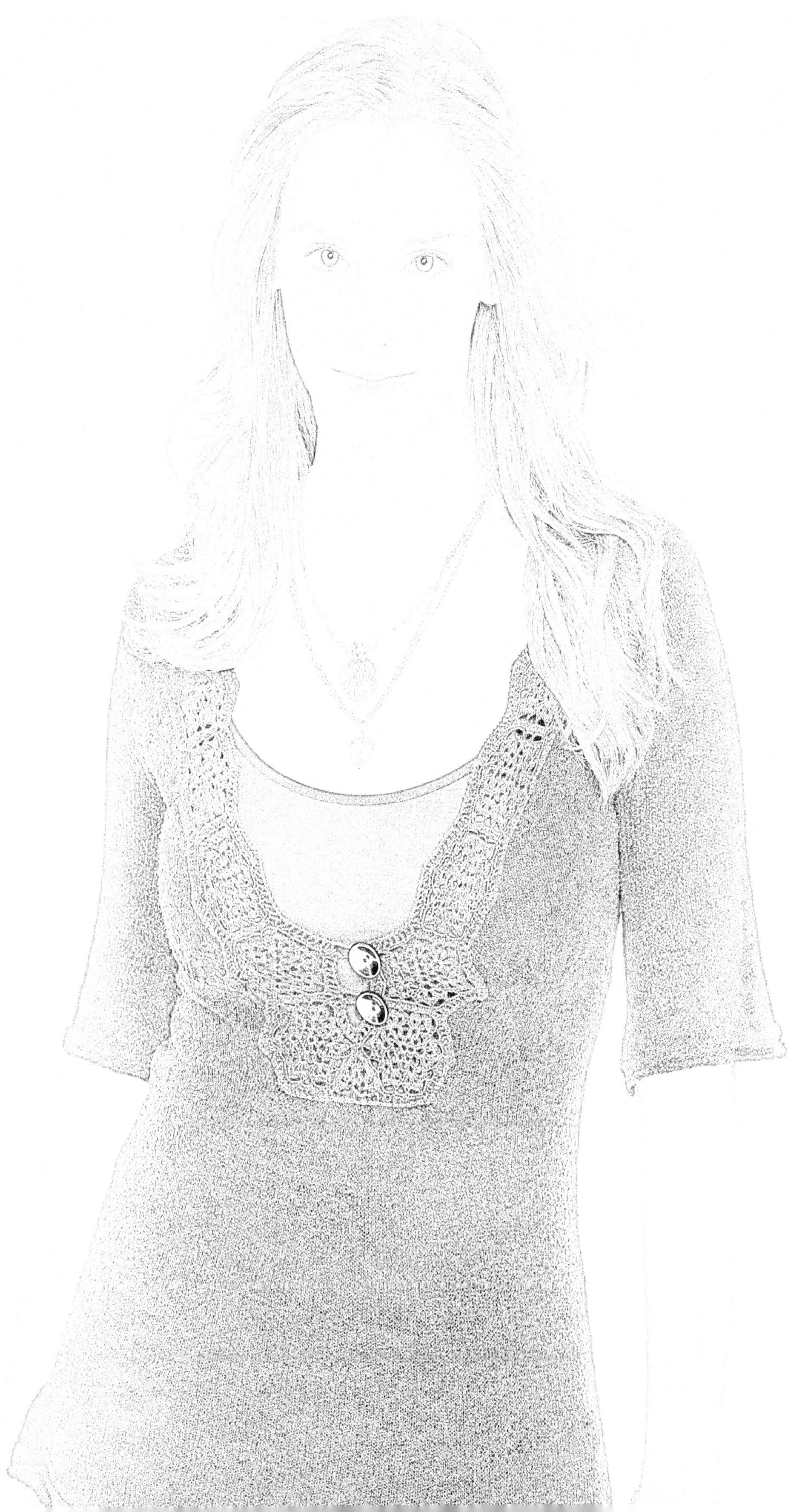

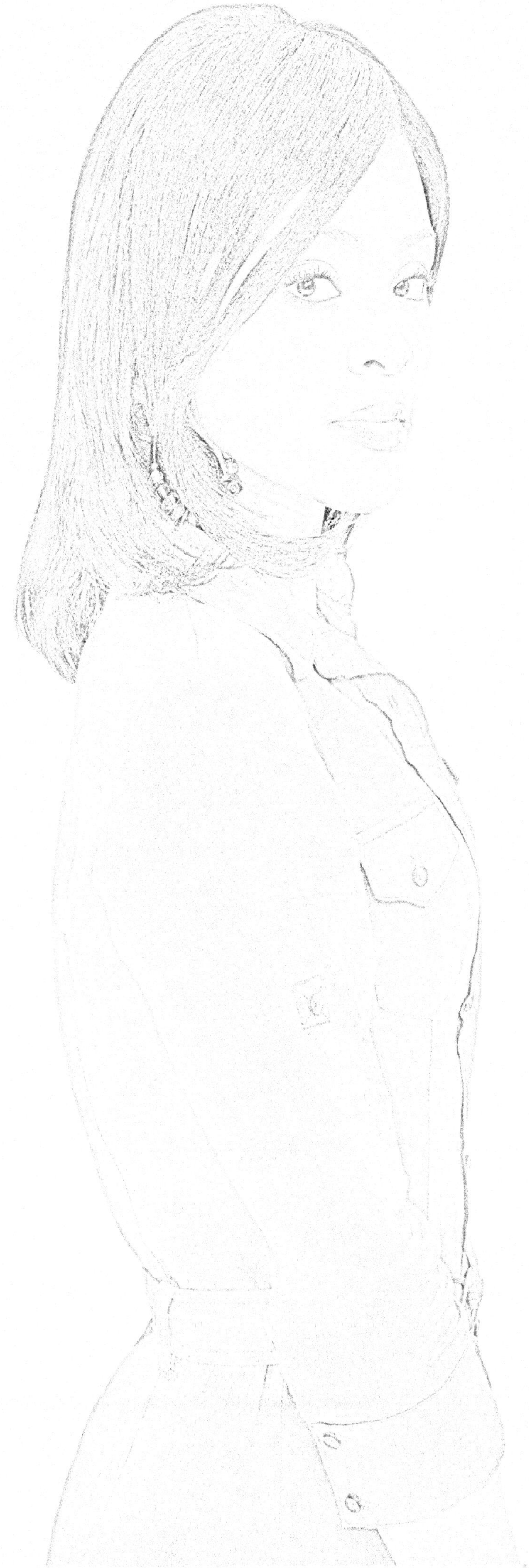

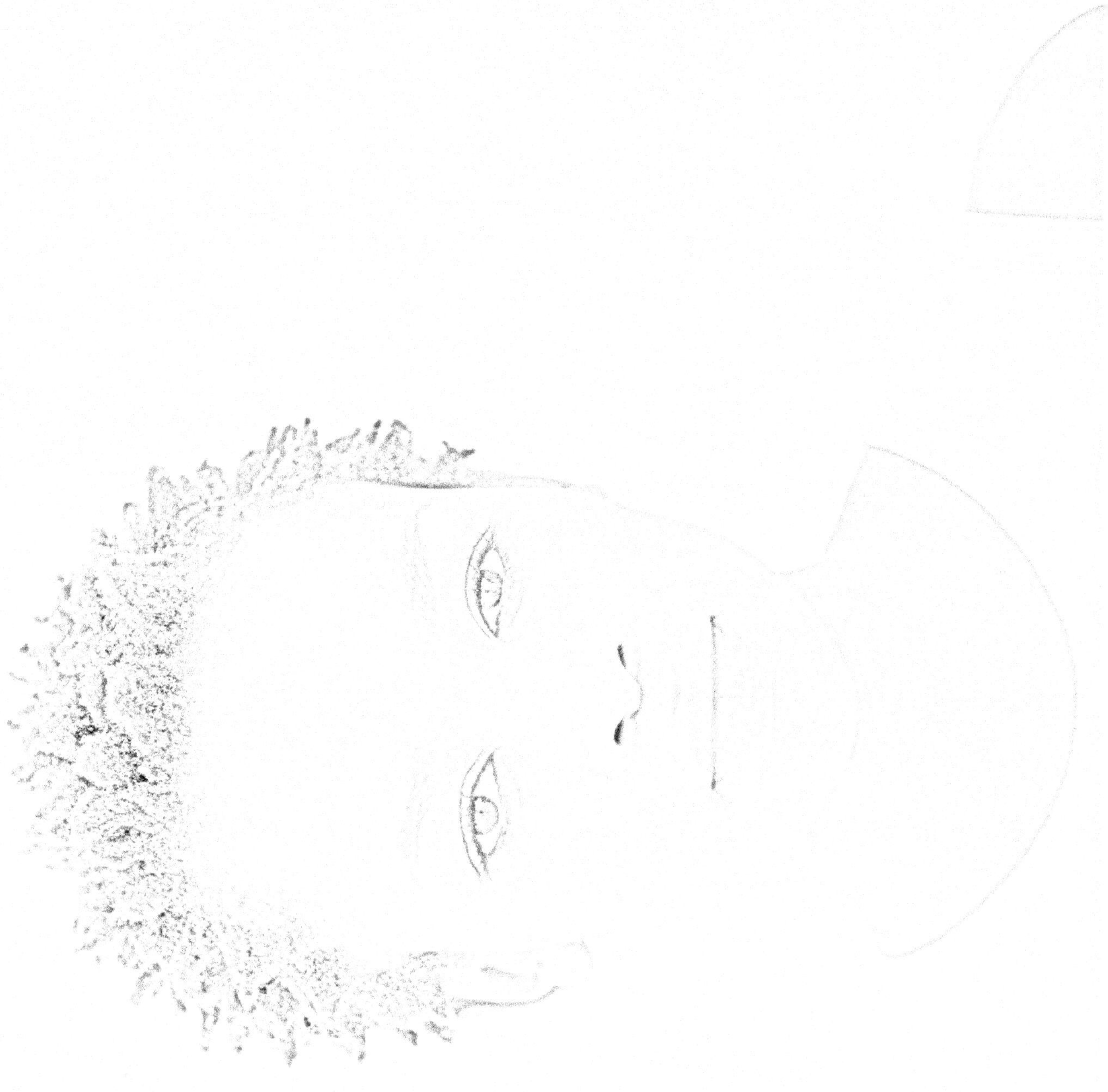

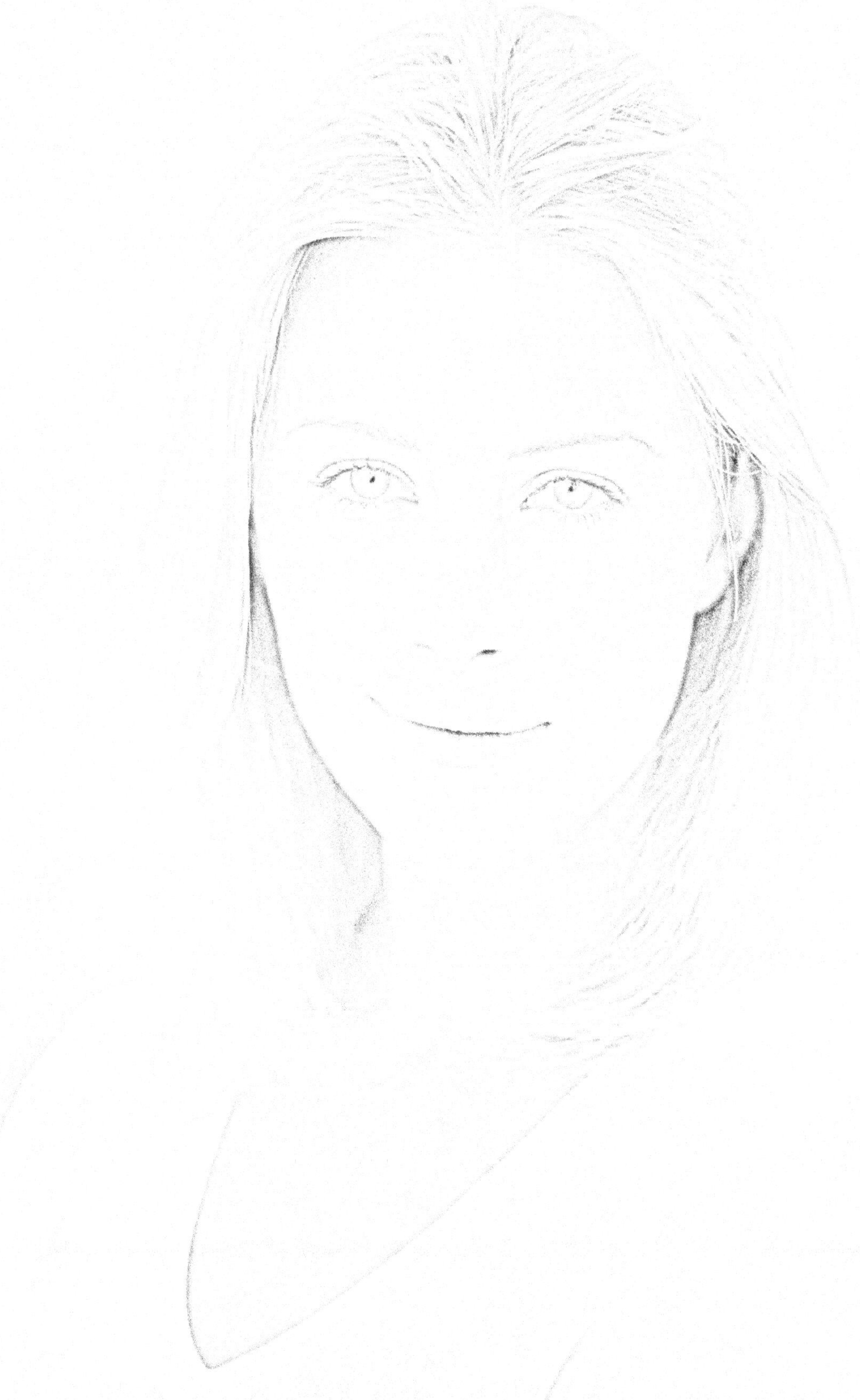

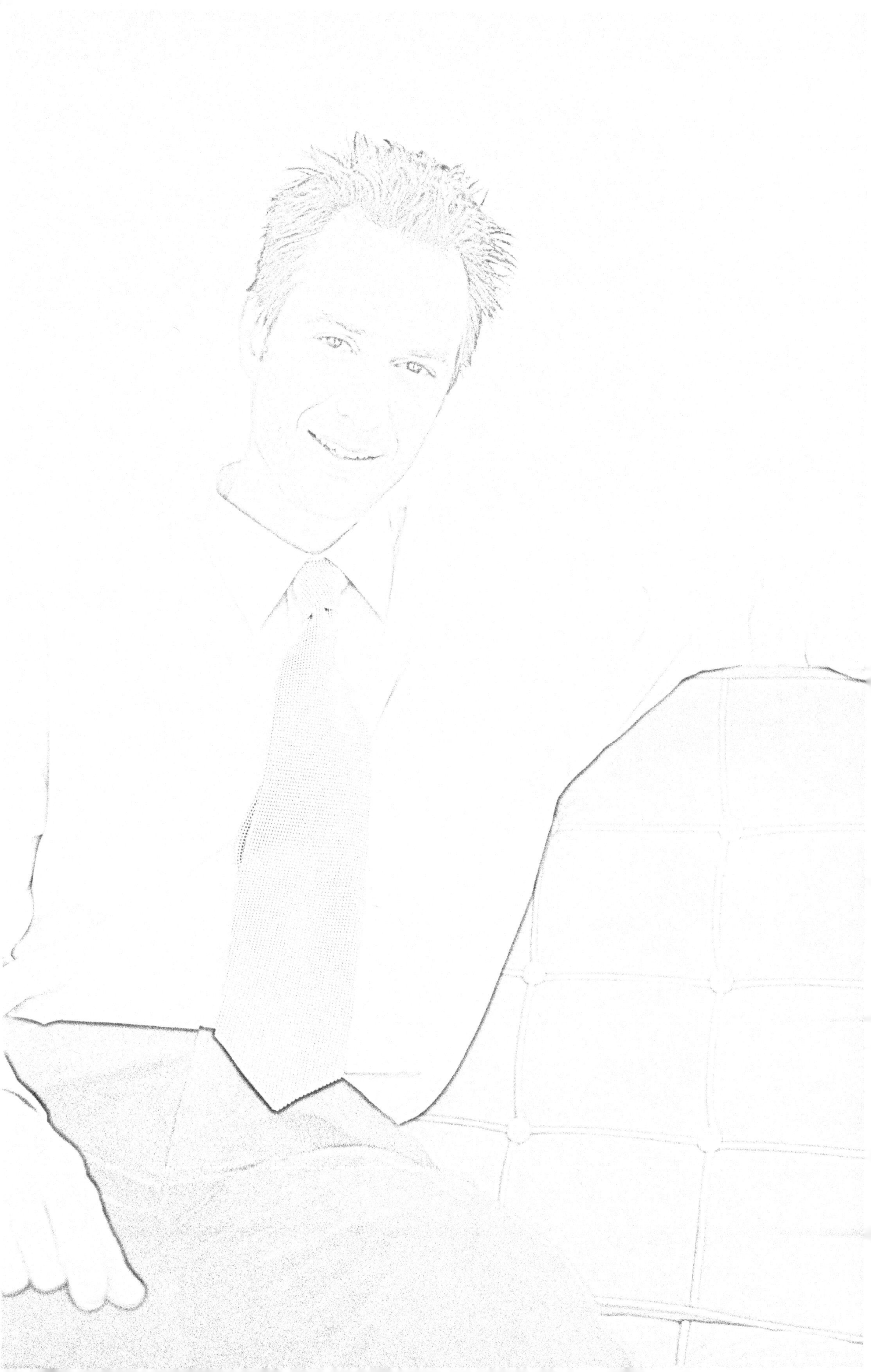

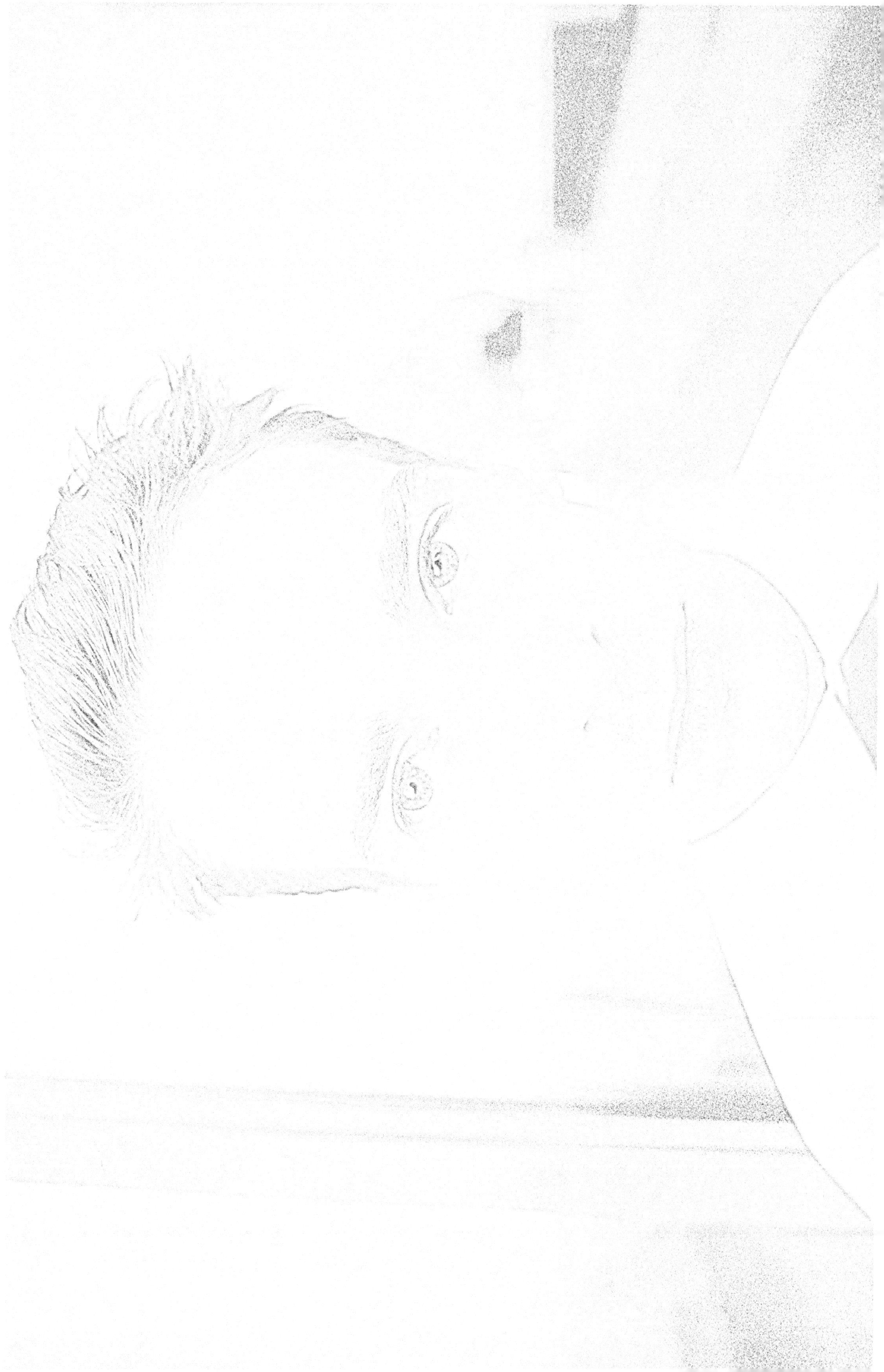

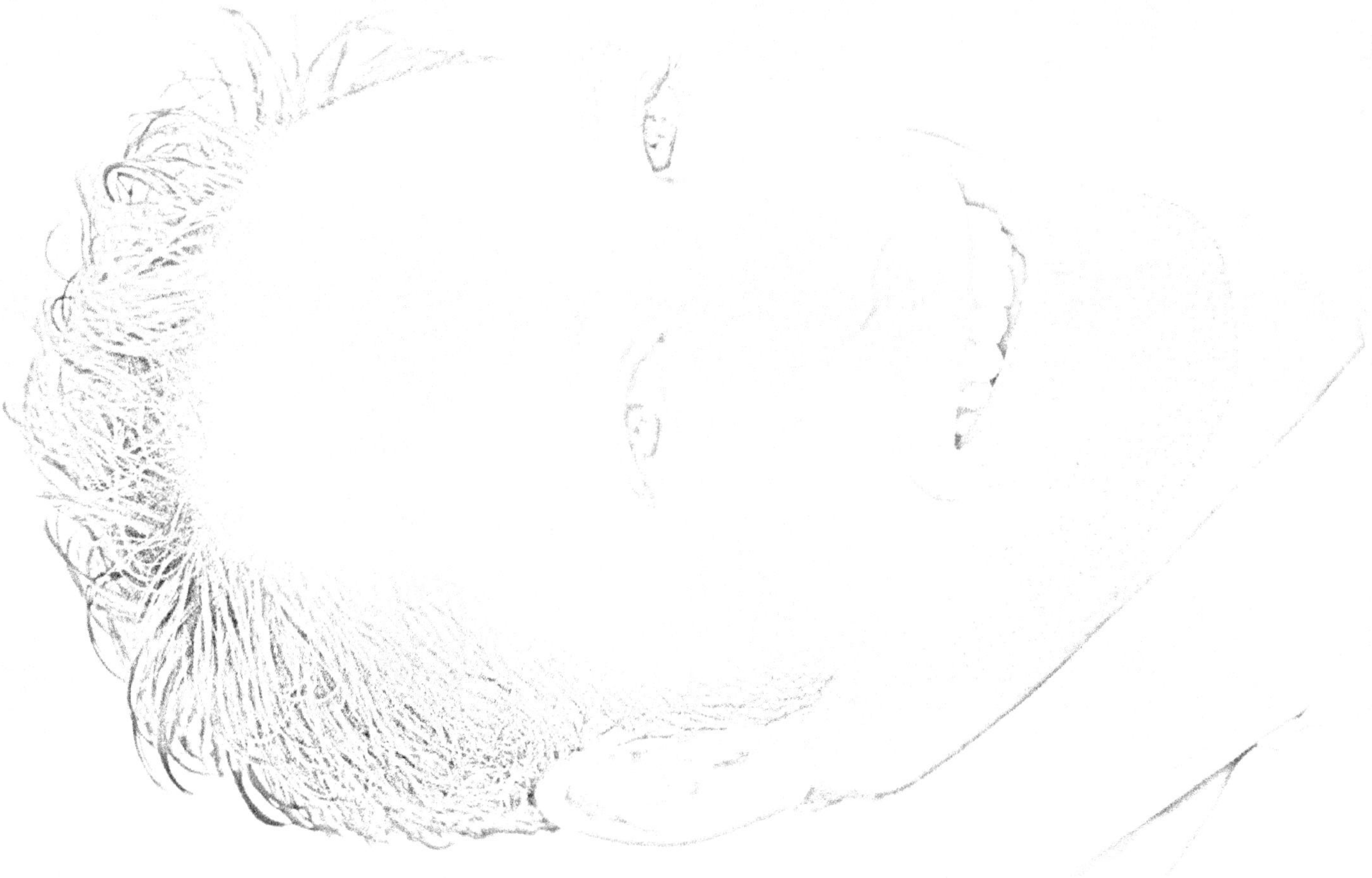

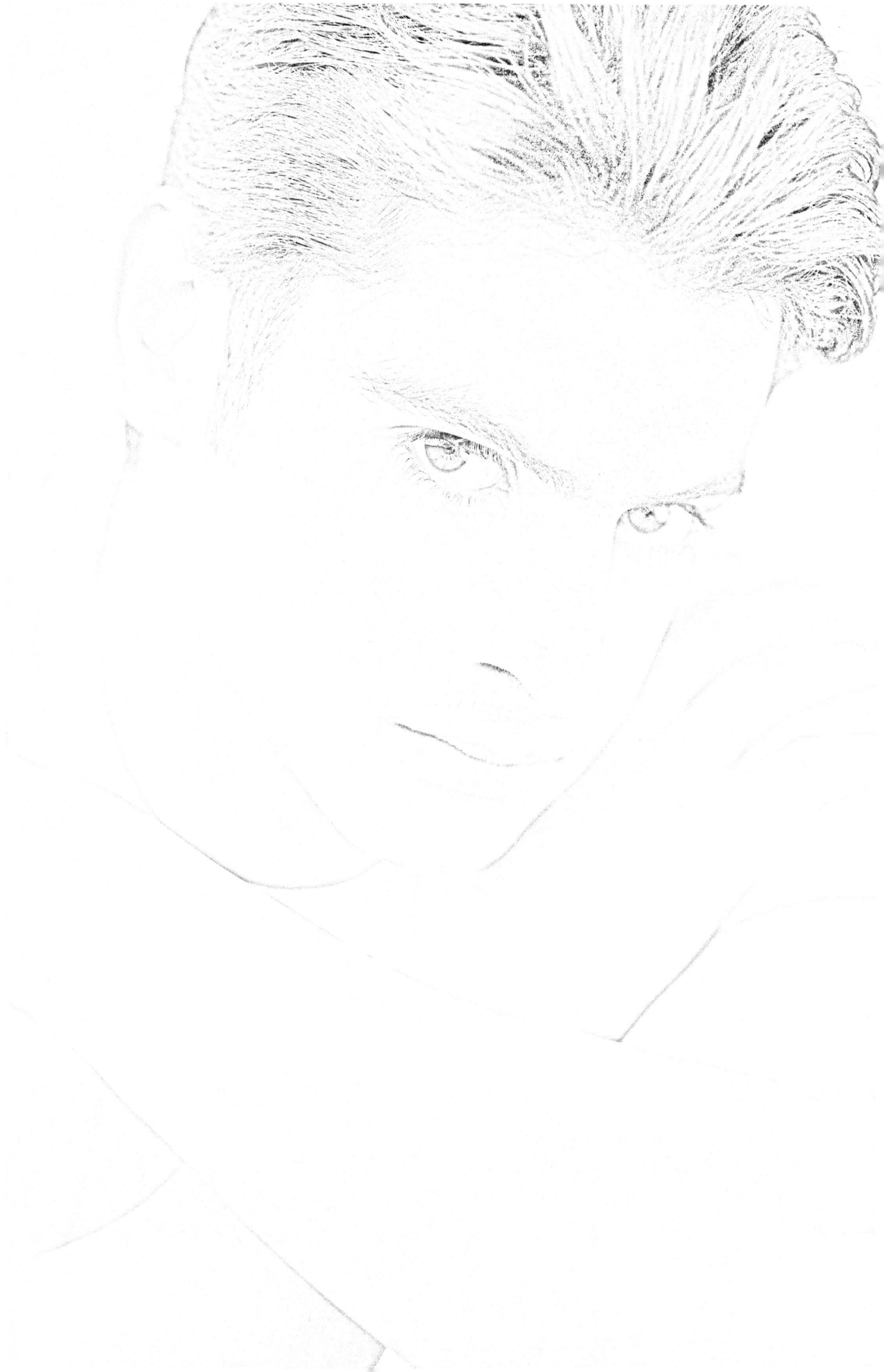

www.ingramcontent.com/pod-product-compliance
Lightning Source LLC
Chambersburg PA
CBHW081057180526
45170CB00005B/1789
* 9 7 8 0 3 5 9 8 6 5 1 5 4 *